THE COMMONSENSE
CHINESE
COOKERY BOOK

By the same author

CHINESE COOKERY
MODERN CHINESE COOKING

THE COMMONSENSE
CHINESE
COOKERY BOOK

Ella~Mei Wong

ANGUS & ROBERTSON PUBLISHERS

All measurements in this book conform to the Metric Cup
and Spoon Measurements of the Standards Association of
Australia.

British and American Readers please note that:
1 metric cup	*250 ml.*
1 tablespoon	*20 ml.*
1 teaspoon	*5 ml.*

Spoon measures are **level** *spoonfuls.*

To my mother
who is still teaching me to cook
and to my family
who always encourage me to write another book

Angus & Robertson Publishers
London • Sydney • Melbourne • Singapore
Manila

First published by Angus & Robertson Publishers, Australia, 1976
Reprinted 1983 by The Thetford Press Ltd., Thetford, Norfolk

© Ella-Mei Wong 1976

National Library of Australia
card number and ISBN 0 207 13317 4

FOREWORD

I look forward, together with all lovers of the Chinese cuisine, to this new book by Ella-Mei Wong as I have been associated with the author for a considerable number of years through her previous books and in the teaching of young professional Chefs at the Food School. This new edition brings fascinating and mouth-watering delicacies, which hitherto have been the treasures only of the Far Eastern parts of the world, within easy reach in the pages that follow.

The author is well respected as an authority on Chinese and Eastern food and with the customs and traditions that are associated with their artistic preparation. She has the ability to write the recipes in a simple, concise fashion with imagination and originality, without losing sight of variety and nutritional aspects. She does not seek to impress the reader with tiresome, complicated instructions, but explains them in her inimitable "easy to understand" approach, and thus continues her original mission to bring valuable knowledge of century old traditions and culture through food, and invites everyone to share in these habits, customs and culinary delights.

J. T. Goodman-Jones, F.A.H.C.I., F.H.C.I.M.A. (London)
Member of the Association Culinaire Francaise
Senior Head Teacher of Commercial Cookery
Food School, East Sydney Technical College.

CONTENTS

ILLUSTRATIONS

INTRODUCTION

Many years ago, in describing the romance of jade, it was written . . . . "In its translucent depths are stored ten thousand mysteries of the inscrutable East."

There is no mystery here, however, because the aim of this book, *The Commonsense Chinese Cookery Book,* is to enable any cook to apply Chinese cookery techniques and methods using everyday supplies purchased from any supermarket, if he or she wishes. For this book I have created and devised recipes based on traditional favourites which fulfil contemporary requirements for meals that are quick to prepare, economical, appetising and nutritionally balanced, as well as including some delicious but rather more complicated dishes for special occasions and those cooks with more time to spare.

Cooking is considered one of the arts, and creativity is what it is all about. So frequently one returns from eating out at a restaurant disappointed with the food, but practise a little yourself, and very soon I can assure you that you will produce your own special version of each dish. You will be able to eat better and more cheaply at home, not to mention the enormous pride and satisfaction you will gain.

One of the secrets of successful Chinese cooking is the timing. A good chef calculates his time to the very second. Colours and textures are preserved. Arrange all the prepared ingredients on a large plate or tray in the order in which they will be cooked. Have the sauce ingredients already mixed in a small bowl, so that the sauce has only to be stirred before adding to the dish. Use pourer lids on the oil and soy sauce bottles. Arrange the seasonings close to your cooking range. If possible, purchase a wock, which is a treasure in the kitchen because of its versatility, and takes little cleaning.

Chinese food has changed a lot in the last few years. With the countless chefs of second and third generation Chinese living outside China, new ways of processing food and new equipment, it is not difficult to understand why this has happened.

My grateful thanks to my good friend, Food Editor, Ellen Sinclair, for her encouragement, and also to the *Australian Women's Weekly* for allowing me to use the photographs.

The outdoor shots and Beggar's Chicken Dish is the work of Warwick Duffy, to whom I am indebted for taking time off to assist me with the photography.

To my husband I make special *kowtows* for the patience shown while instructing me on the calligraphy which appears in the Wine Section. Also, a *kowtow* to Dai Goh for his contribution.

I do hope that I have stimulated your interest in Chinese cookery, and that you will receive as much pleasure and enjoyment from trying out the following recipes, as I have gained in preparing them for you.

ELLA-MEI WONG

THE ART OF CHINESE COOKING

Chinese food can be cooked on any type of fuel with success. It is a well-known fact that for centuries Chinese cooks have used whatever they could find for fuel. They would gather twigs, leaves, wood, in fact, anything that would burn. I have seen dishes for enormous parties cooked in several clay pots over just charcoal and wood. In fact, today, these same clay pots are still used with charcoal in many homes.

With all the modern facilities of luxurious gas and electric ranges there should be no excuse for not being able to manage this style of cooking.

One can quite comfortably go through life cooking food with just the one method that the Chinese call 'chow'. This method is closest to 'saute'. Many cookbooks describe this method of 'chow' as stir-frying. I do not agree entirely, as the action requires using a ladle which has a scoop base of at least 8–10 centimetres square and 'lifting' the food while it is being seared in the hot oil or fat. At the same time, the wock is turned around to ensure that all the food is cooked to the same degree. This is the best reason for cutting all the ingredients into uniform size. When you become adept at handling the wock, there is no need to use the ladle, because you can lift the wock off the heat and toss the food up and down to cook.

Cooking over a high temperature, as required for 'chow', brings out the natural flavour of the food and seals in the natural juices. It is very quick as well. When adding another ingredient, use the ladle and turn the food over to mix. At the last stages of cooking, add the sauce. Then, and only then, is stirring necessary.

It is only experience and practice that will enable you to achieve perfection in preserving the texture of your vegetables. You must learn to sear when necessary and to know the precise minute when the food is cooked to perfection—another minute over this time, and disaster. The 'chow' technique will produce a masterpiece, when you have learned the required temperatures and different cooking times for a variety of foods.

One clue to the success of this method is to discipline yourself to be a master of organisation. Everything must be within arm's reach before commencing to 'chow'. Place the main ingredients for the recipe on a tray in the order of cooking. Blend the sauce ingredients and keep the sauce handy to add at the last minute. You can make a dish that will be pleasing to the eye by chopping or slicing the ingredients so that they are uniform in size.

COOKERY TERMS

Barbecue: Generally means cook over an open fire or charcoal burner over coal.

Baste: Spoon or brush liquid over the food that is being cooked.

Blanch: Plunge into boiling water for a given period of time.

Braise: Brown in a little oil or lard, then cook over low heat with a small amount of water or stock.

Crush: Pound or crush with a cleaver.

Cube: Cut into cubes ($\frac{1}{2}$–2 cm).

Deep-fry: Cook in enough oil to cover food to be fried.

Dice: Cut into $\frac{1}{2}$ cm cubes, or even smaller.

Drippings: The juices that remain from the cooked food.

Flambe: Set aflame with small quantity of warmed brandy.

Garnish: Add to decorate the finished product.

Marinade: The liquor in which food is marinated.

Marinate: Soak in a marinade, usually soy sauce, oil, vinegar and seasonings. The purpose of this is to make the food more tender and give it a special flavour.

Mince: Chop very finely with two cleavers, or put through a mincer.

Mix: Stir together.

Pan-fry: Cook over heat in a little oil or lard.

Parboil: Boil until partially cooked.

Saute: Cook quickly over heat in a little oil or lard (turning frequently).

Shred: Cut into very thin strips (2–3 cm in length).

Simmer: Cook over low heat just under boiling point.

Slice: Cut the food into thin oblong pieces either diagonally or straight across (in size 5 cm by 2 cm). Used mainly for the Chinese chafing dish known as sukiyaki and for hard vegetables.

Soak: Cover completely with liquid for a specified time.

CHINESE COOKERY TERMS

Bie: Presenting or decorating food after it has been cooked; serving food with a garnish to attract the eye.

Bo: The process of boiling, as in *bo farn* or to boil rice.

Chow: Frying quickly in a little oil or lard in a shallow pan, when the ingredients literally jump from the pan; to toss food.

Dunn: Slow cooking in a large earthenware pot over a charcoal fire; for instance, a whole duck would be simmered for hours in this way.

Gook: Baking in an oven.

Gup: The ingredients are first sauteed, then braised in stock and simmered until tender.

Heung sui: A barbecue process which colours the food after it has been seasoned, usually with a thick soy sauce to give it a deep, rich brown colour; a fragrant grill.

Hong: Toasting or grilling.

Jar: To squeeze or extract liquid.

Jin: Lightly fried in butter or oil; term applied to frying whole egg.

Jing: Food is put in a casserole or on a plate, which is placed on a stand in a large pot of boiling water covered with a lid, and steamed gently.

Jow: Frying in sufficient oil or lard to deep-fry.

Jum: Placed in water or liquor to soak or marinate.

Jup: Sauce or gravy of varying textures; drippings from cooked meats.

Yeung: Ingredients are minced or finely chopped to be stuffed in vegetable, poultry or fish.

Yip: To pickle fruit and vegetables, or to salt fish.

METHODS OF COOKING

FAST COOKING
Fast cooking includes frying, boiling and simmering.

Boiling (Bo): Food is boiled in water or stock until cooked.
Deep-frying (Jow): Place enough oil or fat in a deep container to cover the
    food. Cook until golden brown in colour.
Fricaseeing (Mun): Food is first seared in hot oil and then simmered in a little
    stock.
Pan frying, quick frying, stir frying or sauteing (Chow): The food is fried
    quickly in a little hot oil or fat and is turned frequently while browning.

SLOW COOKING
Use earthenware or crockpots over direct heat which is very low. The pots
retain the heat for a long time. Pigeon, squab, grouse and pheasant are
cooked in this way with the addition of medicinal herbs and Chinese wine.

STEAMING
Three methods of steaming are used in Chinese cookery.

Jing: This is one of the quickest ways to prepare food by steaming it on a
    wire rack or stand, which is placed in a large saucepan or wock, filled
    halfway with water. Cover with a lid and, as the water boils, the steam
    circulates and the food cooks gently.
Choy: This is a method of direct or wet steaming. The steam comes in
    direct contact with the food. A bamboo steamer covered with a lid is
    placed in a wock filled with water coming to the base of the steamer.
    More than one steamer can be used by stacking them one on top of the
    other. The Chinese buns, dim sims, glutinous cakes and fish are done this
    way.
Dunn: An earthenware casserole with a lid is placed on a stand which is all
    placed in a larger saucepan half filled with water. This is a very slow
    steaming process and is valuable during very cold winters. The food is
    left mostly in whole pieces, and the steaming process ensures the food
    will be soft enough to be pulled apart with little effort.

STEWING
Chinese know this method as *hoong sui* or 'red cooked'. The food is seasoned
with thick soy sauce, colouring and seasonings and simmered till tender.
The result is a beautiful reddish-brown glaze on the food when it is cooked.

Some utensils useful in Chinese cookery.

ROASTING

Ducks and chickens are hung on hooks over a flame in deep barrel-like ovens. These days modern ovens are used.

BARBECUING, BROILING OR GRILLING

Food cooked outdoors over coals or gas barbecues. Small portable barbecues are very popular. Oven grillers are sometimes used.

ROTISSERIE

The food is threaded on a spit and cooked evenly in a closed oven. Peking duck is threaded on a large fork and turned by hand over coals to resemble a rotisserie.

EQUIPMENT

It is not necessary to have special equipment to cook Chinese food. Any type of frying pan, saucepan, casserole dish or baking tray can be used successfully. Once you master the techniques and become familiar with the particular recipe you want to prepare, it will be comparatively easy for you. You will be able to fry rice in a tin plate!

If you are serious about your Chinese cooking though, then you must acquire a wock. There is no need to buy an expensive one. An ordinary iron one will last you a life time if you take good care of it. The one I am using today cost me three dollars and I have had it over twenty years. It is my constant companion when I go overseas to demonstrate Chinese cooking.

The wock is a pan shaped like a half-circle with two loop handles on the rim. It comes in all sizes with or without a cover. It retains the heat so desirable in Chinese cooking and is easy to handle. It has the added feature of being able to take a bamboo steamer on top.

If your gas or electric range will not accommodate the round base of the wock comfortably, then use a metal ring to steady the wock. Only a plain type is required with enough ventilation allowed in between the wock and ring, so a 'v' cut on the ring stand will suffice.

A Chinese type ladle is necessary, because, with its long handle and scoop base, it enables you to keep turning the food over rapidly when using the 'chow' method. I have many ladles which I have picked up in different parts of the world.

A well-equipped kitchen has cutting knives, cleavers, spoons, casseroles, strainers and chopping boards. These items will all do double duty for you.

A banquet dish—Whole Fillet of Beef with Black Bean Sauce (page 64).

I find that a large baking dish with a wire stand inside will cook any large fish beautifully and I use aluminium foil as a cover. Just brush a little oil on the aluminium foil before covering so it will not touch the fish while cooking. The large dish can be put across two burners on your range.

Of course, no meal would be complete without chopsticks. If you are learning to use them for the first time, I recommend that you start with the wooden ones.

COOKING OILS

The Chinese chef prefers to use vegetable oil or lard in his cooking. When the oil is heated it has a more flowing consistency and, in the very cold weather, it will not congeal in the food thus aiding digestion considerably. Also for people who have to watch their intake of cholesterol, vegetable oil is better than lard or fat.

The Chinese peanut or groundnut oil does not come refined and therefore has to be cooked before it can be used. A crushed piece of garlic, crushed ginger or shallot are added to the oil whilst heating which gives it a fine flavour. This oil can be kept and used when required for salads, dip sauce or just to sprinkle over plain vegetables.

There are many oils on the market. I name them as salad, corn, safflower, soy, olive and sesame oil. It is not desirable to cook with sesame oil alone as it tends to become bitter and burns quickly. Olive oil is a little strong in flavour to be used in Chinese cooking. What is required is a subtle flavour in the food, so therefore, I prefer peanut or salad oil.

Lard is used a lot especially as it is cheaper than vegetable oils. It is better when clarified. It has a tendency to congeal when the food becomes cold, and I feel that it should be used in moderation.

In Eastern countries where coconuts are plentiful, coconut oil is the popular choice because of its price. It takes a little time to become accustomed to this flavour, and I find its aroma rather overpowering.

THICKENING AGENTS

The Chinese chef has at his disposal in a large kitchen many thickening agents for his sauces. They are chestnut flour, lotus root flour, tapioca flour, cornstarch, glutinous rice flour, potato and taro root flour, ordinary plain flour, arrowroot, soy flour and cornflour.

Any of these used in the correct quantities will thicken your sauce, but for convenience in writing the recipes, I have used cornflour blended with water or stock.

To thicken a soup, a liaison of eggs is used, and also any of the flour agents.

ENTERTAINING

CHINESE ETIQUETTE

At an everyday meal in a Chinese family, all the dishes are brought to the table at the same time and each person is served with a basin of steamed rice. Usually there are three dishes and a soup for four adults, and I have planned my recipes for service in this way.

At a formal Chinese banquet the scene changes considerably. This would be held in a large restaurant and there would be ample help, waiters, wine waiters and serving girls (*amahs*). The ideal number is ten and the guest list is planned for units of ten people to a round table. Even the cost of the party is calculated in this way.

The dishes are brought out one at a time and served by the waiters. The menu would consist of at least nine courses, and there is no limit to the courses, depending on the financial status of the Host. Of course, a wedding is a grand affair, and such an occasion calls for great spending. Birthday parties for those 51, 61, 71, 81, 91 and upwards are glad times to celebrate. A party of this type is considered of prime importance to the Chinese to attaining these precious years. A christening party for the child after one month is another cause for celebrating.

At a formal family party a lazy susan table would be used so that it can be whizzed around for all to share the food. It is considered etiquette at these parties for everyone to wait until the Host invites all to start the meal. Also one does not extend a hand over to the other side of the tables for the food, but chooses whatever is in easy access. The turntable is a great invention in this respect, as it is turned around slowly so one can choose without any problem. The Host occasionally will, with the aid of another pair of chopsticks, not the ones he is using, choose a titbit and offer it to the guest. It is considered etiquette if invited for a family meal to wait until the head appears at the table before starting.

I was brought up in a large family and we all waited for Father to come to the table before we would dare start to eat. Then my brothers and sisters and I would devour the dishes each one liked specially without eating enough rice for the filler. For this we would be scolded. This was the environment in which I was brought up, and it may sound old-fashioned now, but it was gracious discipline. I think it is such a pity that it is less frequent nowadays—where have those families gone?

On special occasions when dining out at a reception, there are spiced watermelon seeds and nuts to nibble throughout the meal. In between courses, tea and wines are served too. One therefore can rest between courses, sipping tea, nibbling watermelon seeds and smoke — no wonder it takes hours to sit through a banquet!

When congratulations are to be offered, the Host and Hostess visit each table and many toasts are offered. The Chinese feel that by sipping wine and eating alternately, intoxication is prevented to a degree. It is the custom to hand out fragrant warm towels to the guests in lieu of starched serviettes, which are very practical and refreshing. Piping hot tea is served after a meal and is soothing to the system.

SELECTING A CHINESE MENU

On numerous occasions I have been asked to suggest a menu for a group of friends who want to get together and enjoy a meal in a Chinese restaurant. Each restaurant has its own 'specials' and its own version of classical Chinese dishes, but as a general rule, it is good to strive for variety. Order one dish for each person present, plus a soup. It should all come to the table at once, so that everyone can taste each dish. The only thing served separately would be the steamed rice. Rice takes the place of bread or a roll in a European meal.

In choosing a menu, order a different style of cookery for each dish. For example, try something deep-fried and braised; a dish that has to be steamed and a stir-fry one. Different styles of cutting, dicing, slicing, chopping, mincing give the desired variety to the same main ingredient. It is thus entirely permissible for an ingredient to appear more than once in a menu.

It is advisable to tell the head waiter your preferences, how much you are prepared to spend, and, more important, how much time you are prepared to wait. Below I suggest a few menus which will give a balanced and nutritious meal, and will, I hope, appeal to most lovers of Chinese food.

(1)   Bean Curd Soup (Crab and Lobster)
Steamed Spare-ribs with Sweet Sauce
Crisp Skin Chicken with Prawn Crisps
Beef and Vegetables
Barbecued Pork and Shrimp Fried Rice
Fresh Fruits in a Salad with Ice Cream
Tea   Coffee

(2)   Sweet Corn Soup
Shrimp and Green Peas
Barbecued Pork Flambe
Steamed Bream with Mushrooms
Chicken and Sliced Vegetables
Lychees and Ginger Ice Cream
Tea   Coffee

(3)   Mushroom Soup
King Prawn Cutlets with Crisps
Chicken in Pineapple Sauce
Scallops with Snow Peas
Fillet of Beef with Black Bean Sauce
Lychees Special
Tea   Coffee

(4)   Consomme with Mixed Vegetables
Chicken Roll with Prawn Crisps
Fillet of Beef with Black Bean Sauce
Sweet and Sour Pork with Fried Rice
Baked Snapper
Fresh Fruit — Ice Cream
Tea ·   Coffee

When I was living in Hong Kong in the mid-fifties, it was a fashionable era for entertaining and there were parties each night of the week. Not just the inevitable wedding and birthday parties, but mah jongg and card parties, arrival and departure parties, even nothing-to-celebrate parties. Attending these parties helped me appreciate food to its greatest extent. Each party had a different menu, and was held either at a home or at a restaurant. At a private home, caterers were brought in, so that the Host was always free to enjoy uninterrupted pleasure.

The Chinese banquet menu is different from an ordinary restaurant menu. It may be written in Chinese on a special form and read from right to left. The name of the dish is written downwards in each column provided. In the heading is the name of the establishment, the name of the party giver and the type of celebration, such as birthday or wedding. Some of the courses planned for an evening would read as follows. Note that the sequence of the arrival of dishes is different from other menus.

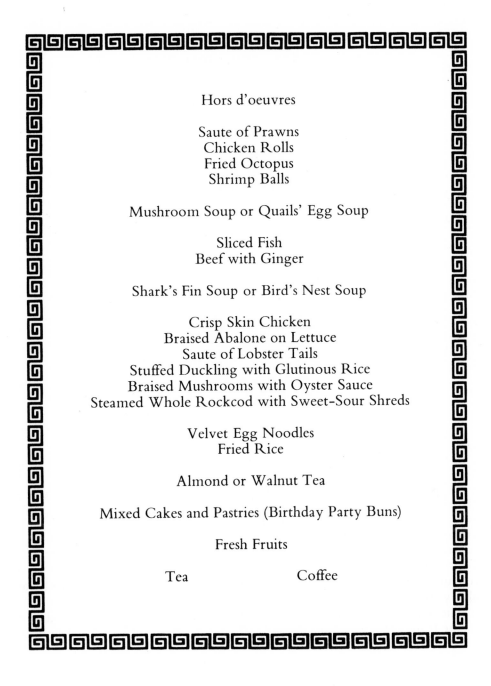

Hors d'oeuvres

Saute of Prawns
Chicken Rolls
Fried Octopus
Shrimp Balls

Mushroom Soup or Quails' Egg Soup

Sliced Fish
Beef with Ginger

Shark's Fin Soup or Bird's Nest Soup

Crisp Skin Chicken
Braised Abalone on Lettuce
Saute of Lobster Tails
Stuffed Duckling with Glutinous Rice
Braised Mushrooms with Oyster Sauce
Steamed Whole Rockcod with Sweet-Sour Shreds

Velvet Egg Noodles
Fried Rice

Almond or Walnut Tea

Mixed Cakes and Pastries (Birthday Party Buns)

Fresh Fruits

Tea   Coffee

ENTERTAINING AT HOME

At some time in the future you will no doubt wish to try out your Chinese-style cooking on your friends.

A buffet is the most practical way of catering for a group, and the easiest for the host or hostess to handle. It is recommended that both hot and cold dishes are served, both for variety and for convenience. The most popular hot dishes are Beef with Black Bean Sauce, Sweet and Sour dishes and Saute of Prawn dishes, which can be made in advance and kept warm. The table or tables should be set out ready, with the cold platters presented, before the guests arrive, to set the mood for the party and to reduce the workload when you are ready to serve dinner.

It is desirable to appoint a friend to take charge of the serving of the food to the guests, and another to take charge of the drinks. In this way the duties of the host or hostess are alleviated and he or she is left free to drift around, seeing that everyone is having a good time.

TO SERVE WITH DRINKS

PORK AND VEAL RISSOLES

250 g pork and veal mince
1 rasher fatty bacon or ham
  fat
Salt and pepper
1 teaspoon soy sauce
1 egg
1 beef stock cube
Cornflour

Mince fatty bacon and mix into the pork and veal mince to make a fine texture. Add salt, pepper and soy sauce. Beat egg lightly in a small basin and stir into the mixture thoroughly.
Break up stock cube and sprinkle over mixture. Shape mince into small balls about 2 cm in diameter and dust lightly with cornflour.
Deep-fry in hot oil until golden brown. Drain on absorbent paper.

Note: When using these tiny rissoles for soup, do not deep-fry.

SAVOURY CHICKEN WINGS

12 chicken wings
Water
2 chicken stock cubes
$\frac{1}{4}$ cup thin soy sauce
$\frac{1}{2}$ teaspoon sugar
1 teaspoon salt
2 cloves crushed garlic
3 tablespoons hoisin sauce
  (substitute honey)
3 tablespoons sweet sherry
$\frac{1}{2}$ cup vegetable oil

Put chicken wings into saucepan with enough water to cover. Add stock cubes. Cover and cook until just tender. Drain.
Combine soy sauce, sugar, salt, crushed garlic, hoisin sauce, sherry and vegetable oil in a bowl. Add chicken wings and stand at least 1 hour, or even overnight, in the refrigerator. Turn over occasionally.
Cover a wire rack with aluminium foil and put into a baking dish. Place chicken wings on wire rack and cook in moderate oven until browned, approximately 20 minutes.

CRYSTAL PRAWN BALLS
Bor Lay Har Kow

1 kg raw prawns (or use cooked prawns)
3 tablespoons sherry
Pinch salt
1 tablespoon cornflour
2 egg whites
1 cup cooked vegetables (cauliflower, green beans, snow peas or broccoli)

Peel shell from prawns and remove intestinal tract. Wash and drain. Pat dry and place in a bowl.
Pour sherry over the prawns. Sprinkle with salt and half of cornflour.
Stir in unbeaten egg white, and sprinkle mixture with balance of cornflour.
Heat oil in wock and when hot, saute the prawns until they change colour and add the vegetables. Continue stirring until vegetables are heated through. If too dry, add 1 tablespoon of liquor from the cooked vegetables.
Serve hot.

CURRY PUFFS

2 dozen 4 cm puff pastry cases
Filling:
400 g minced beef
1 teaspoon salt
1 tablespoon soy sauce
1 onion
1 tablespoon vegetable oil
2 tablespoons curry powder
1 teaspoon curry paste
2 teaspoons cornflour
2–3 tablespoons stock
Mango chutney

Season beef with salt and soy sauce. Dice onion finely and saute in hot oil until transparent. Stir in curry powder and curry paste. Add meat and mix together. Blend cornflour with stock and cook into meat mixture until thickened.
Spoon filling into puff pastry cases and put into moderate oven to heat cases.
Serve hot with a slice of mango chutney on top.

SLICED ABALONE
Bow Yue

1 can abalone
Lemon juice

There are soy sauce flavoured abalone, or just plain cooked ones, obtainable in cans.
To serve as hors d'oeuvres, slice into thin pieces and serve separately with a squeeze of lemon, or add to a tray of mixed hors d'oeuvres.

DEEP-FRIED DIM SIMS

500 g minced meat
1 large onion
1 large slice ham fat
Salt and pepper
2 tablespoons soy sauce
1 tablespoon vegetable oil
1 egg white
Cornflour
250 g noodle pastry skins (see
    recipe below)

Mix minced meat with chopped onion and ham fat. Add salt, pepper, soy sauce and vegetable oil. Stir in the unbeaten egg white.
Wrap 1 tablespoon of mixture firmly in each noodle pastry skin and squeeze together tightly. Sprinkle tops with cornflour.
Deep-fry in hot oil until golden brown.
Serve either hot or cold.

Note: If there is a Chinese delicatessen in your locality, you will probably be able to buy the pastry skins there, already rolled and cut. If you prefer to make your own, here is the simple recipe. I suggest that you make up a batch and keep them wrapped in a sealed package to be used again. They can be stored for 10 days in this way.

Noodle Pastry Skins:
2 cups flour
1 egg
1 teaspoon water
Cornflour

Sift flour on to a board. Make a well and break in the egg. Put in the water and mix into a pliable dough.
Sprinkle the board with cornflour and roll out until pastry is paper thin. Cut into 7 cm squares.

SHRIMP CRISPS

150 g shrimp crisps
Oil for deep-frying

Heat oil in wock and when hot enough, drop the shrimp crisps in gently, a few at a time as they will expand. This process will only take a couple of minutes.
Remove and drain on absorbent paper. Keep in an airtight container.
Note: Test the correct temperature of the oil by dropping in a small piece of shrimp crisp first. It will immediately expand and rise to the top if the oil is at the correct temperature.

MINI SPRING ROLLS

200 g wun ton skins
Filling:
200 g pork and prawn mince
    (or pork/veal and prawn
    mince)
1 tablespoon vegetable oil
1 stalk celery
1 cup bean sprouts or finely
    shredded cabbage
1 tablespoon soy sauce
Salt and pepper

Fry pork and prawn mince in hot oil until it changes colour. Shred celery finely and fry for one minute with the mince. Wash and remove ends of bean sprouts and stir into mixture. Season with soy sauce, salt and pepper. Allow to cool and pour off excess liquor.

Spoon filling on to wun ton skin, and wrap tightly into small parcel. Refrigerate for 1 hour or longer to consolidate filling. Have oil ready for deep-drying and gently fry until golden brown. Drain.

Note: Wun ton skins are available from Chinese food shops and some Chinese restaurants. If unavailable, make up a batch when you have the time and keep wrapped in plastic. They will keep from 7–10 days.

DIM SIMS

500 g pork
200 g shelled raw prawns
6 dried mushrooms
1 large onion
1 large slice ham fat or 2
    tablespoons lard
Salt and pepper
2 tablespoons soy sauce
250 g noodle pastry skins (see
    recipe on p. 17)

Mince pork and prawns together to a fine mince. (Keep a few prawns for decoration.)

Soak dehydrated mushrooms in warm water for 10 minutes. Wash and squeeze dry. Put into a small saucepan with water to cover and bring to the boil. Simmer for 15 minutes. When cool, cut into small dice and add to the pork mixture.

Cut onion and ham fat into small dice and add to the mixture.

Stir in the seasonings, and mix well together.

Place 1 tablespoon of mixture in centre of noodle skin and squeeze together. Top with a small prawn and steam for 20 minutes.

Serve either hot or cold with extra soy sauce.

Note: Water chestnuts and celery can be substituted in lieu of mushrooms and onion. I like the combination of dehydrated mushrooms and waterchestnuts.

SEAFOOD COCKTAIL ROLLS

1 cup cooked seafood (crab, lobster, prawns, scallops)
2 slices ham fat
100 g minced pork
1 teaspoon soy sauce
Salt and pepper
1 teaspoon oyster sauce
Spring roll pastry wrappers

If using crabmeat, remove fibres and separate meat. Cut scallops and prawns into small lengths. Heat wok and fry shredded ham fat until brown, then add minced pork and season. Add seafood and mix well together. Allow mixture to cool.

Wrap filling in spring roll wrappers, sealing ends securely. Place on a shallow casserole and steam for 10 minutes. Pat dry before deep-frying.

When ready to serve, deep-fry in vegetable oil until golden brown. Drain.

SHIMMERING MEAT BALLS

250 g glutinous rice (nor mei fun)
250 g minced pork (or pork and veal mince)
1 large onion
1 tablespoon soy sauce
½ teaspoon salt
½ teaspoon curry powder
1 slice ham fat

Wash and soak the glutinous rice for 1–2 hours. Wash again and allow to drain.

Mince pork and onion together to a fine mince. Season. Mix in chopped ham fat and knead gently until mixture is pliable. Shape into small balls and roll in the glutinous rice. Cover generously.

Prepare a shallow casserole for steaming and place the meat balls so that they do not touch, because in the steaming process they will swell.

Serve either hot or cold.

Note: If fresh water chestnuts are available, use these instead of onion—really delicious!

WHITE TURNIP PICKLES

1 or 2 large white turnips (250 g)
2 tablespoons salt
3 cups vinegar (white)
3 tablespoons sugar
Peppercorns
Dried bird's eye chilis (hot)
¼ cup warm water

Scrape skin from turnips and cut into slices 3 cm long by 1 cm thick. Sprinkle with salt.

Warm enough vinegar to cover turnips in a saucepan. Pour vinegar into a large bowl, not aluminium. Allow to cool.

Put in turnips with sugar, peppercorns and dried chilis. Pour in ¼ cup warm water. Adjust taste.

These will be ready in 2–3 days. Store in clean glass jars with liquor covering turnips.

EGG SPRING ROLL

Pancake:
2 eggs
½ cup water
½ teaspoon salt
½ cup sifted flour

Filling:
1 large carrot
1 stick celery
1 length shallot
1 cup cooked pork, beef, chicken and ham or combination
½ cup cooked shrimps
3 tablespoons minced ham fat (or lard)

Beat eggs, water and salt together lightly in a small bowl. Pour the egg mixture into the sifted flour and beat until smooth.

Grease your omelette pan or a 18 cm diameter frying pan with a little oil or fat and when hot enough, put in enough batter to make a very thin layer on the bottom of the pan. Cook on one side only. Remove and allow to stand on upturned saucer. This mixture should make about 6–7 pancakes.

Clean and finely shred carrot and celery. Parboil in boiling water for 3–4 minutes. Remove and drain. Chop shallots finely and add to vegetables.

Grind or chop very finely the cooked meats, shrimps, and ham fat. Mix with the vegetables. Correct seasoning.

Place 1 large tablespoon of the mixture in centre of cooled pancake and roll up firmly, tucking in the ends securely. Refrigerate for 1 hour to chill and firm mixture.

Deep-fry in moderate heat until golden brown, turning to brown all sides evenly. Remove and drain on absorbent paper.

Serve either hot or cold.

STEAMED PASTRIES
Sui Mei

Skins:
250 g Chinese flour (deng min fun)
2 heaped tablespoons corn-flour
1 heaped tablespoon rice flour
1½ cups water, approximately
2 tablespoons lard

Sift the three flours together and place into large mixing bowl. Boil the water in a small saucepan to dissolve the lard.

Using chopsticks or a wooden spoon, work the hot water into the flours to make a dough. Cover with a damp cloth so the dough will not dry out. When warm, knead gently and make into a long roll.

Break off 2½ cm lengths and using a flat cleaver or small rolling pin which is greased with lard, press or roll into a circle.   *(continued)*

Filling:
300 g pork mince
1 tablespoon vegetable oil
300 g prawns
1 large piece canned bamboo shoot
4–5 cooked mushrooms
2 tablespoons soy sauce
1 tablespoon oyster sauce
½ teaspoon sesame paste
Salt and pepper
1 egg yolk

To make filling, saute pork mince in vegetable oil for 3–4 minutes. Dice prawns, bamboo shoots, mushrooms and add to the pork mixture. Add the seasonings and cook together for a few minutes.

Beat egg yolk gently and stir into the mixture. Allow to cool in refrigerator before using on the pastry.

Place filling in centre of pastry and pinch edges together to form a pleated top.

Place in a greased bamboo steamer or steam by indirect steaming method for 10–14 minutes. This pastry will have a transparent appearance.

CHINESE DOUGHNUTS
Jin Doih

500 g glutinous rice flour (nor mei fun)
2 cups water, approximately
250 g slab brown sugar (or brown sugar)
1 small can soy bean puree (hoong do sar)
½ cup sesame seeds
Oil for deep-frying

Sift flour in a deep bowl and make a well in the centre.

Place slab sugar and water to cover over gentle heat just to dissolve. When cool, pour into flour and work into a soft dough, kneading lightly.

Shape into a long roll about 4 cm in diameter, and break off into 5 cm lengths. Roll between the hands and flatten out into a circle.

Place 1 teaspoon of puree in centre and close up to make a complete round shape. Take off any excess dough and try to keep the dough evenly distributed. Roll in sesame seeds.

Heat oil in a deep pan and deep-fry the doughnuts over moderate heat. When doughnuts rise to the top, press down gently, repeat process till cooked, approximately 10 minutes. Drain on absorbent paper.

These doughnuts should be served within the hour, otherwise they deflate and become very chewy.

SHRIMP BOATS

2 dozen pastry shells (6 cm × 2 cm)

Filling:
500 g raw shelled shrimps
½ teaspoon salt
1 teaspoon soy sauce
1 egg white
4–5 water chestnuts (or 1 small onion)

Chop cleaned prawns to a paste and season with salt and soy sauce. Beat egg white to a stiff snow and fold into prawn mixture. Add the finely chopped water chestnuts.

Spoon mixture with a teaspoon to form a small ball and deep-fry until golden brown. Drain on absorbent paper.

Heat pastry shell in moderate oven till warm. Dip the shrimp ball in mayonnaise and place on pastry shell.

Note: These pastry cases are shaped like a boat. They can be bought in large food stores and cake shops.

PRESERVED EGGS
Pee Darn
(Known as 100 year old eggs)

'Hundred-year-old' eggs are in reality ducks' eggs which are only a few months old. The eggs are covered with a mixture of ashes, tea, lime and salt, rolled in dried rice husks and buried for approximately four months. After this time, they are ready to be eaten. The result of the process turns the yolk of the egg into an orange-green colour, with the albumen solidified into a dark green jelly with white star streaks.

'Hundred-year-old' eggs are eaten with vinegar and ginger or any type of mixed pickles. Served as an appetizer they have a high place in the Chinese diet. One has to acquire a taste for these eggs, but they have a taste so individual as to excite any palate.

Remove the husks and clay from the egg and wash thoroughly. Peel off shell and cut into quarters. Serve with mixed pickles.

Assorted Gow Gees   Top: Crystal Prawn Balls (p. 16) and Shrimp Crisps (p. 17). Bottom: Deep-fried Dim Sims (p. 17), Mini Spring Rolls (p. 18), Potato Balls (p. 66), Steamed Pastries (p. 20).

DRUMSTICKS

12 chicken 'drumsticks'
Chicken stock (use stock cube)
Salt and pepper
1 cup barbecue sauce (Hoisin Jeung or any other brand)
2 eggs
½ cup cornflour
Fine bread crumbs or cracker crumbs
Oil for deep-frying

Home-made Barbecue Sauce:
½ cup soy sauce
3 tablespoons tomato sauce
1 tablespoon tomato puree
1 teaspoon chili or hot tomato sauce (or 1 tablespoon Worcestershire sauce)
4 tablespoons salad oil
1 tablespoon honey diluted in warm water
½ teaspoon salt
Sherry

Boil drumsticks in chicken stock for 20 minutes. Remove, drain and pat dry.
Place drumsticks in a deep bowl. Sprinkle with salt and pepper and pour the barbecue sauce over them. Allow to stand for 30 minutes.
Beat eggs lightly in a bowl.
Sprinkle cornflour over the drumsticks, dip into the egg mixture and then lightly cover with fine bread crumbs or fine cracker mixture.
Deep-fry in hot oil until golden brown, or alternatively, bake in a hot oven for 30–40 minutes.
Serve with pickled cucumbers and garnish with parsley. Can be eaten either hot or cold.

For home-made barbecue sauce: Combine ingredients. A very good sauce, useful if you cannot buy the above brands.

FRIED SHRIMP CAKES

1½ kg fresh shrimps
200 g fatty pork
1 teaspoon salt
1 teaspoon sugar
1 tablespoon soy sauce
1 tablespoon hoi sin jeung
1 egg yolk
½ cup salad oil

Shell and clean the shrimps. Mince with the pork into a fine mince. Add the seasonings. Stir in the beaten egg yolk.
Shape the mixture into 1½ cm thick round or square cakes.
Heat oil in a shallow pan and when hot, fry for 2–3 minutes on each side. Heat for 5 minutes in the oven before serving.

Savoury Chicken Wings (p. 15)

BUTTERFLY SHRIMP TOAST

500 g fresh shrimps
Slices of day-old white bread
250 g fillet of fish
Salt
1 egg yolk
Oil for deep-frying
Shrimp crisps

Peel shrimps and remove intestinal tract, leaving on tail portion. With a sharp knife split the back lengthwise down to the tail end, so that there will be two sections to fan out, like a butterfly.

Cut bread into oblong lengths a little larger than the size of the shrimps.

Pound the fish until it is a fine paste, add salt and stir in the lightly beaten egg yolk. Spread this mixture across the length of the bread and place the butterfly on top. Refrigerate for at least 1 hour before cooking.

Deep-fry in hot oil until golden brown. Drain on absorbent paper. Serve as an appetiser with shrimp crisps.

SOUPS

BROWN STOCK

Any type of meat bones
Soup meat
1 brown onion
Peppercorns
Assorted vegetables and/or
   trimmings

Brown the bones, soup meat and cut-up onion under the griller or fry in a shallow frying pan. Place in a deep saucepan, add peppercorns and chopped vegetables. Cover with water and bring to the boil. Turn down heat and allow to simmer for 1–2 hours.

Allow to cool, preferably overnight. Remove any scum and fat that have congealed on top. Bring to the boil once again.

Strain stock and when cool, store in the refrigerator. This stock can be used as the base of sauces, gravies and soups.

SHORT SOUP
Wun Ton

Noodle pastry skins
250 g pork
250 g raw shelled prawns
Shallots
1 slice ham fat
1 tablespoon soy sauce
Salt and pepper
1 egg

Mince pork, prawns, white ends of shallots and ham fat together to a fine paste. Stir in seasonings. Mix the unbeaten egg white with the pork mince. Place 1 teaspoon of mixture on pastry skin and seal all edges with beaten egg yolk. Fold over to form a triangle.

If using for soup, heat seasoned soup and when boiling, lower the wun tons into the soup. When cooked they will rise to the top.

If using for hors d'oeuvres, deep-fry the wun tons in hot oil until golden brown. Drain.

Note: For *Sweet and Sour Wun Ton*, use deep-fried wun tons with a sweet and sour sauce on top.

CHICKEN STOCK

Chicken carcass, giblets
Pork bones
Peppercorns
Vegetables (white onions, turnips, celery, carrots)
A piece of fresh green ginger

Place chicken carcass and pork bones, peppercorns, cut-up vegetables and green ginger in a large saucepan, cover with water and bring to the boil. Simmer for 1 hour. Allow to cool.
Remove any scum and fat and bring to the boil again.
Strain stock and use as desired. It is not necessary to add salt to the stock, especially if it is to be stored, because the seasoning will be added when preparing dishes required.

LARGE DUMPLING SOUP
Soo Gwo Tong

8–10 dumplings (soo gwo) per person
Chicken soup
Chopped shallots
Soo Gwo:
500 g minced pork (fat and lean)
100 g minced ham
Salt and pepper
1 teaspoon soy sauce
4 prepared mushrooms
Pastry:
2 cups flour
½ teaspoon salt
1 egg
Water

Mix minced pork and ham together, add salt, pepper and soy sauce. Add the finely chopped mushrooms. Stir together to make a fine paste mixture.
To make pastry, sift flour and salt together on a board. Mix the egg into the centre of flour. Use enough water to make into a pliable dough. Knead gently. Divide into two sections and roll out into very thin sheets. Cut pastry into 9 × 9 cm size approximately.
Take 1 tablespoon of pork and ham mixture, spread on pastry and roll up like a parcel. Refrigerate for 1 hour to congeal.
Heat chicken soup and when boiling gently slide in the soo gwo. Cook for 8–10 minutes, and remove with perforated soup ladle to individual bowls. Ladle the hot seasoned soup over the soo gwo and sprinkle with chopped shallots.

Note: This is an authentic Cantonese dish and is a complete meal in itself.

SWEET CORN AND CRABMEAT SOUP

1 small can sweet corn
1 small can crabmeat
Chicken stock (add soup stock
    cube)
1 egg
Chopped shallots

Remove the fibres from the crabmeat and separate into pieces.

Drain the corn and add the liquor to the chicken stock. Heat chicken stock and add corn. Add seasoning to taste.

Beat egg lightly in a small bowl. Just before serving, pour beaten egg through a fork and swirl on top of hot soup.

Ladle hot soup into a bowl, sprinkle with crabmeat and chopped shallots.

BEAN CURD AND SEAFOOD SOUP

200 g fresh bean curd
100 g cooked crab meat
100 g cooked prawns or lob-
    ster meat
½ cup diced bamboo shoots
3–4 abalone (from can)
Chicken stock

Cut bean curd into 3 cm squares. Remove any fibres from crabmeat and shell prawns. Cut abalone into fine strips.

Have a well seasoned rich chicken stock ready in a large saucepan and bring to the boil. Put in the bean curd for 10 minutes. Then add the bamboo shoots, crab meat and prawns and cook for 5 minutes.

Serve in a large soup tureen, ladling the hot soup and contents into the bowl. Sprinkle with the shreds of abalone.

BEAN CURD SOUP
Dow Foo Gung

150 g fresh bean curd
100 g cooked barbecued pork
1 small can water chestnuts
1 piece of bamboo shoot
100 g crab or lobster meat
8 dehydrated mushrooms
    (large)
Chicken stock

Cut the bean curd, the barbecued pork, water chestnuts and bamboo shoot into small dice. Remove any fibres from crabmeat.

Wash mushrooms and cover with water. Boil for 20–30 minutes. Remove and when cool, cut into small dice.

Have rich chicken stock on the boil. Put in bean curd, and cook for 5 minutes, then add all the rest of the ingredients. Adjust seasoning to taste.

Serve in soup tureen or separate bowls.

CHICKEN AND POTATO SOUP

1 whole chicken, chicken pieces and/or pork bones
1 onion
1 carrot
Celery pieces
Peppercorns
12–15 new potatoes
1 tablespoon salt
Chopped shallots

Place chopped vegetables and peppercorns in a large saucepan with water to cover. Bring to the boil.
Clean chicken, chicken pieces and/or pork bones and put into saucepan and cook until tender. Remove chicken and bones.
Peel potatoes and add to strained chicken stock. Season with salt. Cook until potatoes have disintegrated. Adjust liquid if necessary.
Serve soup with shredded chicken meat and chopped shallots.

Note: If using whole chicken, reserve half of chicken meat for other dishes.

WHITE TURNIP SOUP

1 large white turnip
200 g lean pork
4 shallots
Rich stock
Salt and pepper
1 tablespoon soy sauce
4 tablespoons brandy

Peel turnips and cut into thin slices approximately 3 cm thick. Slice pork into thin slices. Chop shallots.
Heat stock in a large saucepan and add the turnips and pork. Season to taste. Simmer 15–20 minutes or until turnips are tender.
Before serving, stir in soy sauce and brandy. Serve in a deep soup tureen and sprinkle with chopped shallots.

EGG FLOWER SOUP

Clear chicken stock (or make stock with chicken stock cubes)
Salt and pepper
2 eggs
2 tablespoons chopped shallots

Bring chicken stock to the boil. Season with salt and pepper.
Beat eggs lightly in a small bowl. Pour the beaten egg slowly through the prongs of a fork, moving the fork so that the egg covers the surface of the soup. Stir gently to form flower pattern.
Pour the hot soup in a soup tureen and sprinkle with chopped shallots.

Note: The soup is enriched with an addition of chopped ham.

FLOATING PALETTE CHICKEN SOUP

2 large chicken breasts
½ teaspoon salt
150 g fresh shrimps
¼ cup pork fat
1 egg white
1 tablespoon cornflour
Rich seasoned chicken stock

Palette:
3 egg whites
Strips of shallots
1 mushroom
1 slice ham (cut into strips)

Remove bone from chicken and with a cleaver pound breast to make a flat pancake shape. Sprinkle with salt.

Peel the shrimps and chop finely together with the pork fat. Place in a small bowl, and stir in the egg white and cornflour.

Spread this mixture on top of each chicken breast. Place on a shallow plate and steam for about 6–8 minutes, or until chicken is tender. Allow to cool, then cut into squares.

Place the chicken squares in soup tureen. Pour boiling chicken soup over squares. Float palette on top of soup.

For palette, beat egg white until stiff and put on a flat plate that has previously had a little oil brushed on top. Decorate with mushroom, shallots and ham. Steam for five minutes.

MUSHROOM SOUP

2 large pork chops
Soup vegetables (onion, celery, carrots)
10 dried mushrooms (substitute champignons)
10 red dates (hoong joh)
6 lengths dried bean curd (foo jook), optional
Salt and pepper
1 beef stock cube

Place pork chops in a large saucepan with cut-up soup vegetables. Add water and bring to the boil. Simmer for 30 minutes. Remove pork.

Prepare mushrooms by soaking and washing, then cut into 4 pieces. Add mushrooms, red dates and bean curd to soup.

Cut pork up into pieces, and return bone to the soup. Simmer another 30 minutes. Return pork to soup and allow to cool, preferably overnight. Next day remove the fat skin on top of soup. Discard bone.

Season soup with salt and pepper. Sprinkle in a beef stock cube. Heat through and serve steaming hot.

Note: Sometimes the soup is served separately in individual bowls. The ingredients are served on another platter, thus making two dishes.

VEGETABLES

TECHNIQUE IN VEGETABLE CUTTING

Much importance is given to the cutting of vegetables and other ingredients. The cutting-up is the most essential part of the advance
preparation. Usually the main ingredient determines the cut and shape of
the vegetable that accompanies the dish. For example if the meat is cut into
long lengths, then the accompanying vegetable will be cut into similar
shapes. This will ensure even cooking of all the ingredients. In a menu, a
main ingredient can be repeated several times, using different size cuts in
each dish.

Also, as chopsticks are the only implement used in eating Chinese style,
the prepared food must be tender enough to be manipulated with the
chopsticks and of a size that can be handled comfortably.

In the Chinese cuisine, there are five basic ways ingredients can be cut:
1. straight cutting
2. criss-cross cutting
3. rolling criss-cross cutting
4. dice cutting
5. cutting into rounds

Prepared vegetables which are cleaned and peeled are placed in a neat pile
alongside the meats on a dish in readiness for cooking. The vegetables must
remain colourful, flavoursome and still retain their own individual charac-
ter. The Chinese technique of cooking vegetables ensures that all these
qualities remain.

The vegetables may be cut in any of the above mentioned ways to suit the
dish that is being cooked, but usually those vegetables regarded as hard and
semi-hard are cut criss-cross and rolling criss-cross or shaped into rounds.
For a guide, I list below the most well-known vegetables:

Hard vegetables: broccoli, cauliflower, carrots, potato, pumpkin,
yams, swedes and string beans

Semi-hard vegetables: bamboo shoots, melons, celery cabbage, snow peas,
lotus root, mustard top, cabbage, turnips, peas,
chokos, fresh asparagus, fresh corn, root ginger

Soft vegetables: bean sprouts, chilis, peppers, lettuce, cucumbers,
eggplants, Chinese parsley, leeks, mushrooms,

okra, shallots, chives, onions, radishes, spinach, watercress, tomatoes, water chestnuts, vegetable marrows and squash

Most of these vegetables are found in the local supermarket or market garden and can be used happily in Chinese dishes. Learning to master the skill of cooking vegetables the Chinese way (considered the best in the world — ask any connoisseur of food) will benefit you in many ways. Apart from the ease of preparation and the saving in gas or electricity, the full flavour of the vegetables is retained. And in this health-conscious era, the vitamins are retained instead of being poured down the sink.

Basically the method is simple. When cooking vegetables alone, swirl them around in hot oil, flavoured with garlic and green root ginger, or the ends of shallots or onions. Then add the seasoning with a touch of soy sauce. For the hard vegetables that take longer to cook, add a sprinkling of a stock cube dissolved in a little water, which makes the vegetables more tasty. The oil gives the vegetables a rich gloss which makes for smoother eating.

One of my favourite ways to cook vegetables is as mentioned above adding a little chopped smoked ham or bean curd (foo yue), and sprinkling with toasted sesame seeds or toasted nuts. Delicious!!

CHINESE VEGETABLES

It seemed that once Chinese vegetables were exclusive to the Chinese kitchen, but today, they are available to everyone. If these special vegetables are not available, substitute ones of similar texture, that are easily obtained from your green grocer. I give below a list of substitutes that are most useful for experiment and which I find most successful.

Fresh water chestnuts: green cooking apple, use a ball scoop and sprinkle
    with little castor sugar
    choko or green paw paw, dice
    white stalks of celery, dice
    white onion, cube

Fresh bamboo shoots: canned bamboo shoots
    white onion
    white stalks of celery
    white stalks of cauliflower
    swede turnips
    zucchini
    white turnips
    chokos
(The above are especially successful when cut into matchstick lengths.)

Chinese celery cabbage and
Chinese cabbage: outer green leaves of lettuce,
    especially a garden fresh one
    inside tender part of celery
    endive
    head cabbage

Yams: sweet potato
    potato

Bean sprouts: celery hearts
    chokos
    marrows
    zucchini
    white cabbage leaves
    white turnips
} cut into shreds

Fresh lotus root: dried lotus root
    sweet potato
    swedes
    potatoes

Olive nuts: slivers of almonds

CHINESE VEGETABLES

The following are only a few of the better-known vegetables used in Chinese Cookery.

CELERY CABBAGE *(wong ah bark)* comes in two varieties and has a stalk which resembles celery, although it is not hard or crisp. The leaves are pale green to creamy in colour with the texture of lettuce. Celery cabbage is delicious when both the stalks and leaves are shredded wafer thin and served with a vinaigrette dressing. When cut into lengths from 2 cm to 10 cm it is used in saute, braised and soup recipes. When selecting your cabbage choose one which has tightly formed leaves.

CHINESE SPINACH *(bark choy):* the Chinese name for this vegetable actually means white cabbage because of the long white stems. The leaves are a brilliant green colour and when the vegetable has reached maturity, a sprig of tiny white-yellow flowers appears on the top of the centre stalks. This is a very popular vegetable and used in practically all dishes which require vegetable of this type in the recipe. To prepare bark choy separate the white stalks from the leaves, and then cut the stalks into lengths and then sections. Slice the leaves into lengths. Wash thoroughly, drain and cook the white stalks first, as the leaves require a shorter time in cooking. The flowers are eaten also.

MUSTARD TOP CABBAGE *(dai choy)* is a large deep-green coloured vegetable with hard stalks. It has a slightly bitter flavour and is used mainly for soups. When this cabbage is fermented in a brine the bitter flavour disappears, and the green colour deepens. The cabbage is washed thoroughly after three or four days, and then either chopped into dice or shredded. It is a classic accompaniment to any meat dish. The stalks are also used for the making of pickles.

CHINESE CABBAGE *(gai larn)* is a long tender green leaf vegetable with thin stalks which are curved to form a round shape. It also has a sprig of tiny yellow flowers on the centre stalks when fully matured. This is another popular vegetable, and is used in all types of dishes, especially the noodle ones. When this vegetable is young, there is no need to peel off the fibres.

Simply cooked with any vegetable oil, soy sauce and seasonings, it becomes a gourmet dish in its own right.

CHRYSANTHEMUM VEGETABLE *(tong oong choy)* belongs to the chrysanthemum family and the green leaves are the same shape as those of the chrysanthemum. A small edible bud is often attached to the stem. One has to acquire a taste for this vegetable, and it is used in saute and braised dishes. It becomes a speciality vegetable when used in 'Dar Bin Loo' (Steamboat).

CHINESE PARSLEY *(yin say),* a delicate pale green leafed vegetable, has a wonderful, fragrant aroma, and can be used in numerous ways as ordinary parsley. It is comparatively easy to grow and different varieties go under the names of 'coriander' and 'cilantro'. The small round seeds are also ground and used in cooking.

WATERCRESS *(say yoong choy)* is cultivated in slow running shallow water or found in natural surroundings where the streams filter through. It has a slightly peppery flavour and this unique taste is preserved by using watercress in salads, or as a garnish. When using watercress for soup, separate the stalks from the tiny clusters of leaves and cook the stalks first, so that the 'watercress' flavour will permeate the soup. The sprigs of leaves are added at the last moment.

CHIVES *(gow choy):* The slender green shoots are similar to those of winter shallots, except they are flat, and when fully matured have a purple flower. The green shoots only are used in egg dishes, thick soups, rice dishes and Chinese Hot Pot. Chives have an onion flavour and can be used in dishes that require an 'onion' taste.

GREEN ROOT GINGER *(geung),* the fresh root from the ginger plant, is used extensively in Chinese Cookery. The silvery-brown skin is easily scraped away and when the ginger is very young it is paler in colour, crisp, and without any fibres. It is used sliced, diced, shredded, chopped and minced in all dishes, as it is one of the basic seasonings. The taste is slightly hot and spicy, and becomes milder during the cooking process. Do not substitute any other type of ginger for fresh unless the recipe calls specifically for it, but rather omit the fresh ginger completely. Ginger can be stored in the cool part of the refrigerator with other green vegetables.

SNOW PEAS, HOLLAND PEAS, CHINESE PEAS OR SUGAR PEAS *(hollandoe)* are fully edible. The pale green pods are eaten, as well as the peas inside, once the tips and strings have been removed. Just before the pea pods appear on the vines, the delicate stalks and leaves are used as another vegetable which has a wonderfully delicate sweet flavour much in demand especially for seafood dishes.

LONG BEANS *(dow gock):* are very long thin green beans approximately 30–40 cm long. Just cut off the tips, then section into short lengths and cook as for ordinary beans. Some types are thinner than others and consequently firmer in texture—these are the more desirable to the gourmet.

BEAN SPROUTS *(narr choy)* are sprouted from tiny, olive-green mung peas. They can be grown in 48 hours in summer but take longer in the winter months, unless grown under controlled conditions. They add texture and a unique flavour to many dishes and should not be overcooked, so that they remain crisp. They are available in cans but have to be drained before being used, and lose their crispness. Another type of bean sprout is sprouted from the soy bean. It is larger and coarser in texture.

BITTER MELON, BALSAM PEAR *(fooh gwah)* is a type of green cucumber with thick wrinkled skin approximately 1 cm thick. Inside is a spongy pulp of red seeds which is spooned out and discarded. This vegetable owes its bitter taste to its quinine content, and one must acquire a taste for it. In one classical Cantonese dish the fooh gwah is stuffed with pork seasoned with prawn paste and mushrooms and then steamed or braised. The canned fooh gwah is a very good substitute for the fresh.

GOURD *(see gwah)* is also known as Chinese okra or Chinese squash. This gourd is similar to a long cucumber with grooves along the skin, and tapering in at the top. To prepare the gourd, peel all the green skin away and then cut into halves, lengthwise. The flesh can then be cut into oblique slices or pieces. These are used in soup and saute dishes. Being a soft vegetable, the gourd needs little cooking time, and it is most delicious.

BAMBOO SHOOTS *(dook soon),* the root of the bamboo plant, is best when young because then it is not stringy but crisp and tender. It is kept under water when fresh at the markets, but more familiar to most people are the canned shoots, already cooked and seasoned and to be used immediately. Cut the bamboo shoot into slices or pieces, or shred, and they add an exotic touch to your dishes as well as a distinctive flavour.

WATER CHESTNUTS *(mar tai)* are small bulbs which are grown in selected muddy ponds and provide a magical combination of sweetness and crispness. Peel the dark skin away and what remains is a white-creamy vegetable which can be used in numerous ways in all Chinese food. It can also be eaten raw. Canned water chestnuts are a good substitute when fresh ones are not available.

BRAISED CELERY CABBAGE

1 bunch celery cabbage (wong ah bark)
4–5 dried mushrooms (substitute champignon)
1 piece fresh young ginger
2 tablespoons vegetable oil
Salt and pepper
½ cup stock (use soup cube)
3 tablespoons rose wine (mui gway lo)
2 tablespoons cornflour
1 tablespoon soy sauce
1 teaspoon sesame oil
1 tablespoon minced cooked ham

Cut cabbage into two parts, the green leafy sections and the white stalks. Cut into 8 cm lengths, separating the soft leaves from the white stalks. Wash thoroughly and drain.

Soak mushrooms in warm water for 20 minutes, squeeze dry and cut into lengths. Peel skin from ginger and shred finely.

Heat wock and put in oil. Swirl around to heat evenly and saute green leaves for 2–3 minutes. Remove to warm platter.

Saute the mushrooms, stalks and ginger for 2 minutes, add salt, pepper, stock and rose wine.

Reduce heat and return the green leafy parts. Cover with a lid and braise for 5 minutes.

Blend cornflour with little water, add soy sauce and sesame oil. Add sauce to vegetables and cook until thickened and transparent.

To serve, spread the leafy parts on warm platter. Arrange the white stalks in the centre. Sprinkle the minced ham over the top. Serve hot.

SWEET AND SOUR CABBAGE

Half a head of cabbage
1 teaspoon peppercorns
1 tablespoon vegetable oil
2 teaspoons salt
2 tablespoons sugar
1 tablespoon soy sauce
3 tablespoons vinegar
½ teaspoon sesame oil
12 small bird's eye chilis

Cut cabbage into medium size pieces. Wash and drain thoroughly.

Crack peppercorns into small particles.

Heat oil in wock and fry peppercorns for a few seconds, then add oil and fry cabbage very quickly for 3-4 minutes.

Stir in salt, sugar and soy sauce. Cook a further one minute.

Mix vinegar and sesame oil together, and stir through the cabbage. Heat the small chilis through the cabbage.

Keep stored in an earthenware jar and serve cold.

Note: Bird's eye chilis are very tiny and very, very hot.

CABBAGE WITH BACON SHREDS

1 small green head cabbage
1 teaspoon salt
3 rashers streaky bacon
2 cloves garlic
2 cm piece green ginger
½ teaspoon sugar
½ cup stock (use stock cube)

Shred cabbage finely, wash well and drain. Sprinkle with salt.
Remove rind from bacon and cut into shreds. Fry gently and remove to platter.
Put oil in wock or frying pan, and when hot, add crushed garlic. When garlic browns, remove. Put in cabbage, shredded ginger, and sugar, turning as the cabbage is frying. Add stock, then bacon and cook a further 2 minutes.
Serve on heated platter accompanied by fried rice.

ASSORTED VEGETABLES

200 g broccoli
1–2 carrots
½ teaspoon sugar
½ teaspoon salt
1 small can champignons
1 small can bamboo shoots or
   1 small can water chestnuts
3 tablespoons vegetable oil
½ teaspoon sesame oil
Sauce:
1 cup vegetable stock (from
   brocccoli plus stock cube)
2 tablespoons soy sauce
2 tablespoons cornflour
3 tablespoons rose wine

Peel fibres from broccoli and cut into thin lengths. Remove flowerets and break into small pieces. Wash thoroughly. Peel carrot and cut into slices of similar size.
Put the hard stalks, carrot and flowerets on top in a saucepan with a little water, add sugar and salt. Boil for 5 minutes, remove and allow to stand another 5 minutes in the water to cool. Drain.
Drain champignons and bamboo shoots. Slice bamboo shoots to uniform size of other vegetables. Heat oils in wock and saute broccoli stalks, carrot, champignons and bamboo shoots for 5 minutes. Then add the flowerets and stir-fry constantly.
Pour in the sauce mixture and cook until thickened.
Serve hot with any other main dish.

BRAISED LETTUCE

1 head lettuce
2 cloves garlic
1 tablespoon vegetable oil
½ teaspoon salt
¼ cup stock
½ teaspoon light soy sauce

Separate lettuce into leaves and wash thoroughly. Crush garlic.
Heat pan, add oil, salt and crushed garlic. When garlic begins to brown, put in lettuce. Saute for 1 minute, then add stock.
Cook a further 2 minutes then remove to serving dish. Sprinkle with soy sauce.

PUMPKIN IN BLACK BEAN SAUCE

800 g ironbark pumpkin
2 cloves garlic
2 tablespoons vegetable oil
1 tablespoon black beans
1 teaspoon salt
1 teaspoon sugar
1 tablespoon sherry
2 tablespoons soy sauce
½ teaspoon sesame oil
1 cup water or stock

Remove skin and seeds from pumpkin and cut into pieces.
Crush garlic, place in deep saucepan with oil and fry pumpkin lightly.
Place black beans in a bowl, wash, then squeeze dry. Mix in salt, sugar, sherry, soy sauce, sesame oil, water or stock.
Pour over pumpkin, cover with a lid and cook until tender.
Serve in deep bowl sprinkled with chopped parsley.

Note: This is an adaptation from a classical dish using green pawpaw.

BEAN SPROUT AND SALAMI SALAD

3 cups bean sprouts
200 g salami
Dressing:
One part lemon juice to three
    parts salad oil
Salt to taste
½ teaspoon mustard
½ teaspoon sugar
½ teaspoon sesame oil
½ teaspoon soy sauce

Remove ends from bean sprouts and wash thoroughly. Plunge into boiling water for one minute. Remove and drain. Place bean sprouts in salad bowl and arrange sliced salami on top. Chill in refrigerator.
Mix all ingredients for dressing together preferably in a bottle until well blended.
When ready for serving, pour the dressing over the salad.

SHALLOT FLOWERS

1 bunch shallots

Cut off roots and cut shallots into 5 cm lengths. With a razor blade or small sharp knife, cut each piece 3-4 times from end, but be careful not to cut right through. Stand in a bowl of cool water. The longer they are allowed to stand, the curlier they will become.
The shallots can be stripped completely off to use as a garnish also.

Assorted Chinese vegetables: Top row, left to right:
Watercress, Chinese spinach, bean sprouts, mustard top
cabbage. Middle row: Celery cabbage, winter melon,
green ginger root, shallots. Bottom: Butter melon.

GREEN CUCUMBER FANS

Green cucumber

Cut off both ends of the cucumber and rub the exposed ends with this section. This prevents the bitterness sometimes found in cucumbers. Wash well.

Cut cucumber into halves lengthwise and scoop out seeds. Cut each half into 2 or 3 sections on the bias. With a sharp knife make several slashes through each section almost to the edge. Fold each alternate strip into a curve and tuck down on the uncut edge.

About ten strips are desirable, then there will be five strips and five folds. Top the centre with a red cherry.

BROCCOLI IN BROWN SAUCE

1 small bunch broccoli
1 piece bamboo shoot, canned (or substitute white onion)
1 cup chicken stock
1 tablespoon soy sauce
1 tablespoon oyster sauce
2 tablespoons vegetable oil
1 clove garlic
1–2 tablespoons cornflour
2 tablespoons Chinese wine or sherry

Separate flowerets and stems from broccoli. Peel the fibres from the stems and cut into small slices. Parboil stems for 3 minutes then put in flowerets and cook a further 3–5 minutes. Drain.

Cut bamboo shoots into slices.

Heat stock, soy sauce and oyster sauce in a small saucepan.

Put oil in wock and brown crushed garlic. Remove. Put in the broccoli, bamboo shoots and fry together for 1 minute.

Pour in the sauce from the small saucepan and allow to heat through. Cover with a lid for 3–4 minutes.

Mix blended cornflour with wine or sherry, add to vegetable and cook until thickened.

Butterfly Prawns (p. 45).

FISH AND SHELLFISH

There are no restrictions as to the methods of catching fish. In the early ages fish nets were extensively used and as the industry grew, bamboo poles, lines and bait, even cormorants were used in this thriving industry, which had expeditions all the year round.

The lengthy coastline of China, its rivers and lakes, pools and artifical pools, where both fresh-water and salt-water fish are bred, provide a valuable source of food to augment the scarcity of meat, which, in general, is common to the Orient. In this modern age, it is indeed a wondrous sight to behold from the air the endless array of junks and fishing vessels wending their way home at sunset each evening.

Thus the variety of fish and shell-fish is endless. The most well-known types eaten in Chinese cuisine are carp, sea bass, bream, schnapper, perch, salmon, sole, jew fish, mandarin fish, ling fish, garopa, rock-cod and mullet. In general, the type of fish to be used in the recipes will be the larger, coarse-fleshed fish for shredding and mincing, firm-fleshed fish for steaming or baking and fine-fleshed varieties for grilling or frying. The shellfish most eaten are shrimps, prawns, crabs, sharks' fins, lobsters, clams, oysters, beche-de-mer, abalone and scallops.

The Chinese chef is a genius in the preparation and cooking of seafood. Through long experience he has learnt to minimise the 'fishy' taste and smell by using different seasonings and pickled vegetables, cooking the fish in hot oils clarified with fresh green ginger and garlic cloves. He uses a variety of cooking methods including steaming, deep-frying, poaching and marinating.

Serving the fish whole with the head and tail intact ensures that the natural juices are retained during cooking. A whole fish makes a more attractive looking dish when presented. Also there is a certain amount of delicate food in the cheek of the fish, if your taste is so inclined.

Fish should be cooked so that the flesh is moist and leaves the bone readily. One of the most successful ways of achieving this texture, especially if the fish is very fresh, is by steaming with shreds of fresh green ginger or shallots, seasonings, a few slices of mushrooms, bacon or ham. Bring the fish to the table still sizzling with a hot vegetable oil and soy sauce poured over it. This is an easy recipe and so delicious!

PRAWNS, commonly known in some countries as shrimps or scampi, are probably the most popular of all the shellfish. Of course there is no substitute for the fresh ones you have caught yourself, but if you need prawns for your Chinese recipe the frozen ones are very convenient. Today with quick-freezing, numerous varieties are available already peeled and shelled, cooked or uncooked, in various sizes from the tiniest to the king size, and some are even breaded ready for frying. On large packages, the number of prawns per pack or per pound is given to enable the chef to calculate according to his recipe.

The flavour of prawns is so popular that they are found in wafer crisps and in noodles. They are also pounded together mixed with different spices and made into paste. The king size prawns are dehydrated and threaded on bamboo skewers, and can be stored for months and months. When required for use, they are usually steamed with vegetable oil and soy sauce, and eaten as an appetizer.

When preparing prawns, devein and wash them thoroughly. To devein the prawn, use a small sharp knife and make a shallow slit lengthways, with the back facing upwards. Remove the vein, which is the intestinal tract, and wash well under the tap. Pat dry and put aside until ready for cooking.

DRIED SHRIMPS *(har mei)* are tiny shrimps shelled and dried, and used extensively in Oriental cookery. They have a completely different taste and texture to fresh shrimps, but do make any Chinese dish using them most distinctive. Before use gently wash them in cold water, then soak for 20 to 30 minutes in warm water. The left-over liquor can be used for making a special sauce.

PRAWN PASTE *(harm har),* also known as *blanchan,* are tiny shrimps pounded together with spices and made into a highly flavoured paste. This is one of the essential ingredients used in Indonesian-Chinese recipes. The well-known nasi goreng (fried rice) has *harm har* added to accentuate the flavour of the rice. This paste may be steamed over rice when it is cooking and used as an appetiser. It certainly has the ability to lift a jaded appetite. Its counterpart is anchovy paste.

LOBSTERS AND CRABS are not used in everyday dishes and only certain restaurants would choose to serve them. Lobsters are expensive, because of the fact that the young are hatched only every other year. Still the gourmet demands lobster and lobsters' tails are considered a delicacy. If you are fortunate to have lobsters at your disposal, substitute them in a recipe for crabs. I prefer to have my lobsters and crabs alive until ready for cooking. In the females of the species, the eggs or 'coral' are a gourmet's delight. Frozen or canned crab is an excellent substitute for fresh, and a lot more easy to use.

OYSTERS *(hor see).* The Chinese oyster is used in classic Chinese dishes. The large ones are dehydrated and threaded on skewers in series of five or six to a skewer for storage. They are a dark, brownish red colour and must be soaked for long periods, preferably overnight, before use. They can be found in Buddhist and other religious fasting dishes. Oyster sauce *(hor yo),* made from Chinese oysters, is a favourite of all lovers of Chinese food. This sauce is tasty in meat dishes or can be used as a dip. It is readily available in bottles from Chinese delicatessens.

ABALONE *(bow yue)*, also known as mutton fish, is found on the western coast of the USA and along the Mexican coast. This fish is very large and pounded very hard before it is barbecued on hot rocks. The dehydrated fish are brownish red in colour and need to be soaked overnight in warm water. Wash thoroughly to remove any sand, scrubbing with a small brush if necessary. They are eaten as an appetizer and in soup dishes. The ever popular abalone is considered of gourmet class and always included in a gala banquet. The abalone is braised and served on top of a soft, green vegetable with a thick, transparent sauce.

HOME-MADE SAUCES. I list below two simple and inexpensive sauces which harmonise perfectly with fish and meat dishes, I also include a recipe for oyster sauce.

HOME-MADE SATE SAUCE

½ cup peanut butter
½ teaspoon chili powder
½ teaspoon salt
1 tablespoon lemon juice
1 tablespoon soy sauce
½ teaspoon sugar
½ cup water
½ cup vegetable oil
1 beef stock cube

Mix all the ingredients together and heat in a small saucepan. Keep stirring all the time. When cool, store in an airtight jar. Stir before using, as the oil should separate and come to the top.

QUICK SWEET AND SOUR SAUCE

1 large ripe tomato
½ cup sugar
1 stock cube dissolved in ½ cup water
3 tablespoons vinegar
1 tablespoon soy sauce
½ teaspoon salt
1 tablespoon vegetable oil
4–5 sweet gherkins
4–5 pieces sweet preserved ginger
2 tablespoons cornflour

Cut tomato into quarters and put into a saucepan with the sugar, stock, vinegar, soy sauce, salt and oil. Cook over a slow heat stirring all the time. Remove the skin of the tomato. Add the shredded gherkins and sweet ginger. Blend cornflour with little water and cook into the sauce.

HOME-MADE OYSTER SAUCE

A good supply of fresh oysters or bottled fresh oysters
Salt and pepper
Cayenne pepper
Soy sauce (thick type preferable)
Anchovy paste

Thoroughly wash the oysters and drain. Reserve the liquor.

Chop the oysters up roughly, and put into a small saucepan with the liquor and a little extra water to cover. Bring to the boil and simmer for 20 minutes. Season with salt and pepper.

Mash the oysters through a very fine sieve, and discard the residue.

Place the sieved oyster liquor in the saucepan and add approximately 2 tablespoons soy sauce and 1 teaspoon anchovy paste to each half cup of liquor. Return to the heat and boil for 5 minutes. Reduce heat and simmer for 10 minutes. Allow to cool and store in a warm clean jar. Seal and place in the refrigerator.

GARLIC KING PRAWNS FLAMBE

20 king size prawns
2 egg whites
6 cloves garlic
½ teaspoon salt
2–3 tablespoons vegetable oil
½ cup stock
2 tablespoons cornflour
2 teaspoons soy sauce
1 teaspoon hoisin sauce
1 teaspoon tabasco or tomato paste

Cole Slaw:
1 cup shredded cabbage
½ cup bean sprouts
1 tablespoon shredded onion

Dressing:
2 tablespoons lemon juice
3 tablespoons oil
½ teaspoon salt
¼ teaspoon sugar

Shell prawns and remove intestinal tract. Wash and pat dry. For economy, cut each prawn in half, lengthwise. Place in a bowl and mix in the egg whites.

Mince garlic with salt until very finely mashed.

Heat oil in wock and when hot, saute the prawns until they turn pink. Remove to warm platter.

Add a little more oil if necessary, and fry the garlic. Pour in stock, blended cornflour, soy and hoisin sauces, and tabasco. Cook until thickened. Return prawns to heat through again.

Have platter with cole slaw ready (recipe below), and serve the prawns on top. Serve immediately. Flambe with brandy at table.

Mix dressing and pour over mixed shredded vegetables.

SAUTE OF PRAWNS IN TOMATO SAUCE

10 fresh king size prawns
1 clove garlic
1 piece green ginger
1 tablespoon oil
2 small green cucumbers
1 small can champignons
2 thick slices of cooked ham

Seasoning Sauce:
1 cup stock (use stock cube)
½ teaspoon salt
2 tablespoons cornflour
2 tablespoons tomato sauce
1 teaspoon soy sauce
½ teaspoon sugar
½ teaspoon sesame oil or vegetable oil
½ teaspoon hot tomato sauce

Peel prawns and remove vein. Wash thoroughly and cut into 4 pieces. Fry in hot oil with crushed garlic and shredded ginger. Remove to platter.
Peel off most of the skin of cucumber and cut with rolling cut (see p. 30 on cutting vegetables). Place in a bowl and sprinkle with salt.
Drain champignons and retain liquor for the sauce. Cut half of ham into slices and mince the balance.
Prepare the seasoning sauce in a bowl.
Stir-fry the cucumbers, champignons and ham in a little oil and add the sauce, stirring constantly until thickened. Add the sauteed prawns and heat thoroughly.
Serve on a warm platter and sprinkle with finely chopped ham.

SHRIMP BALLS

500 g shelled raw shrimps
Salt to taste
1 rasher streaky bacon
1 egg white
Oil for deep-frying
2 teaspoons soy sauce
Black pepper

Chop shrimps to make a fine mince. Season with salt. Remove rind from bacon and mince finely.
Beat egg white in a bowl until stiff and thoroughly blend in the shrimp and bacon mixture.
Heat oil in a deep saucepan and when hot, take teaspoons of the mixture and drop them into the hot oil. Brown evenly and drain on absorbent paper.
Serve with a dip sauce made from soy sauce and black pepper.

BRAISED BUTTERFLY PRAWNS

1 kg king size prawns
3–4 rashers of bacon
2 eggs
Cornflour
2 tablespoons oil
Rice wine (or sherry)
Lettuce

Peel prawns, removing intestinal tract. Wash thoroughly and pat dry.
With a sharp knife split halfway through prawn to tail end, lengthwise. Press into cornflour. Cut bacon into lengths approximately the size of prawn.

(continued)

Beat eggs lightly in bowl. Dip prawns in this egg wash and press the strip of bacon on to the back. Dip the bacon side into the egg wash again.

Heat oil in a shallow pan and fry prawn on both sides. Cook until puffed approximately 4 minutes, then sprinkle with the rice wine, cover with a lid and cook for another 2–3 minutes.

To serve, shred lettuce onto platter and place the butterfly prawns on top.

SILVER THREAD CHOKOS WITH SHRIMPS

1 large choko
1 teaspoon salt
1 tablespoon vegetable oil
2 tablespoons stock
1 small can cooked shrimps
Toasted cellophane noodles

Sauce:
½ cup stock (from stock cube)
2 tablespoons soy sauce
1 tablespoon cornflour
½ teaspoon salt

Peel and wash choko, then slice wafer-thin across largest surface. Cut into match-stick slices.

Put choko threads in a basin with enough water to cover, add salt. After 10 minutes, wash off salted water and put into a bowl of cool water for 10 minutes. Remove and drain thoroughly.

Heat oil in wock and fry choko threads for 1 minute. Add stock and shrimps, stirring briskly.

Mix sauce ingredients together, add to choko threads. Cook until sauce is thickened. Serve over toasted cellophane noodles.

BUTTERFLY PRAWNS

15 fresh king size prawns
2 egg yolks
1 tablespoon milk
3 tablespoons cornflour
Salt
2 rashers bacon
Vegetable oil for deep-frying

Shell prawns leaving on tail. Carefully cut each prawn down the back and remove intestinal tract. Using a very sharp knife split prawn lengthwise in half, taking care not to cut right through. Press cut side gently with cleaver to flatten.

Beat egg yolks, milk and cornflour together. Season with salt. Cut bacon into 5 cm × 1 cm strips.

Holding tail-end of prawn, dip in the egg mixture, and put strip of bacon on cut side. Refrigerate at least one hour before cooking as this helps the bacon strip hold to the butterfly prawn more securely.

Heat oil in a deep saucepan, and deep-fry prawns until golden brown. Serve with a lemon wedge and sprig of parsley.

GARLIC PRAWNS

500 g fresh king size prawns
Oil for deep-frying
6 cloves garlic
1 large onion
1 stock cube dissolved in ½ cup brandy
2 tablespoons brown soy bean paste (min see jeung)
1 tablespoon cornflour

Peel and remove intestinal tract from prawns. Wash thoroughly and cut into 3 sections. Pat dry and deep-fry in hot oil until they turn pink. Drain. Chop garlic cloves finely and fry in a little oil for 2–3 minutes. Add chopped onion and cook until transparent.

Mix stock cube with water, add minced brown bean paste. Pour over onion and cook a few minutes.

Return prawns to heat through. Add the blended cornflour and cook until thickened.

Serve with plain boiled rice.

STIR-FRY SHRIMPS AND GREEN PEAS

250 g small frozen raw shrimps
2 tablespoons cornflour
½ teaspoon salt
1 egg white
2 tablespoons sherry
3 tablespoons vegetable oil
1 tablespoon finely shredded ginger
100 g green peas
1 tablespoon cornflour
2 tablespoons vegetable stock
½ teaspoon sesame oil

Defrost raw shrimps and place in a bowl. Sprinkle with cornflour and salt. Stir in the egg white and sherry.

Heat oil in wock and put in ginger shreds. Saute prawns until they turn pink, then add the green peas. Cook for 3–4 minutes, stirring all the time.

Blend cornflour and stock together with sesame oil. Add to shrimps and cook until slightly thickened and translucent.

Serve immediately.

BREADED PRAWN RISSOLES

500 g raw prawns
1 rasher fatty bacon
Salt and pepper
1 egg
4–5 slices stale white bread
Oil for deep-frying

Mince the prawns and fatty bacon together. Season with salt and pepper. Beat egg gently and pour into prawn mixture. Gently knead together to form a paste. Shape into rissoles approximately 4 cm in diameter.

Cut the stale bread into small dice. Roll the prawn rissoles into the diced bread to cover evenly.

Heat oil ready for deep-frying. When sizzling hot, deep-fry until golden brown. Drain.   *(continued)*

Note: If the prawn rissoles can be refrigerated for 1 hour before cooking, the diced bread will adhere more effectively.

PRAWN TOAST

500 g raw prawns
Salt and pepper
1 onion
1 egg
1 teaspoon soy sauce
Oil for deep-frying
Stale white bread

Shell, devein and wash prawns thoroughly. Chop into a fine mince. Season. Place in a large bowl.
Chop onion finely and add to prawns. Stir in unbeaten egg white and soy sauce.
Cut crusts off bread and cut into small shapes. Spread with prawn mince and dip into beaten egg yolk. Allow to stand for 15 minutes in refrigerator before deep-frying.
Heat oil in wock and when hot, deep-fry the prawn toast with the prawn side downwards until golden brown. Drain on absorbent paper.
An alternative is to press a strip of ham or bacon into the prawn mince before dipping into the beaten egg yolk.

SATE PRAWNS FLAMBE

20 king size prawns
1 piece green ginger
2 cloves garlic
2 tablespoons vegetable oil
200 g fresh bean sprouts

Sate Sauce:
2 tablespoons sate sauce (purchased in jars or see recipe p. 42)
1 teaspoon soy sauce
½ cup stock (stock cube)
1 teaspoon hoisin sauce

Shell prawns down to the tail end. Remove intestinal tract. Wash and pat dry. Crush ginger and garlic cloves.
Heat oil in wock and put in ginger and garlic. Fry together for one minute then saute the prawns. Discard ginger and garlic.
Pour on the sate sauce, cover with a lid and simmer for 5 minutes. Take wock off flame. Pour warm brandy over prawns and flambe.
Wash and cut off both ends of bean sprouts and blanch in hot water for 3–4 minutes. Remove and place on oyster platter, or flat platter with a small container in the centre.
Place prawns on top of bean sprouts. Ignite the lemon essence over cube of sugar in centre cup and serve.

Note: An oyster platter is a round silver platter with a small holder in the centre about 3 cm in diameter. Soak a cube of sugar in lemon essence, place in the holder and ignite.

BAKED SNAPPER

2–3 kg of fresh snapper or similar fish
2 teaspoons salt
1 piece fresh green ginger
2 cloves garlic
1 tablespoon sweet paste
3 tablespoons preserved vegetable (choong choy)
2 tablespoons soy sauce
4 lengths shallots
½ cup vegetable oil

Clean and wash snapper (remove head if desired). Make 3–4 cuts on top side of the fish. Sprinkle inside and outside of fish lightly with salt. Place on aluminium foil ready for baking on a rack.

Peel green ginger and shred finely. Crush garlic cloves. Spread sweet paste over fish and sprinkle with ginger and preserved vegetable. Add garlic cloves. Half cover top with foil.

Put in baking dish and add enough water to come halfway. Simmer on top of range, allowing approximately 10–15 minutes per pound of fish.

Remove foil and gently ladle fish on to warm platter. Pour liquor from cooking of fish over the top and then spoon on the soy sauce. Decorate sides with shallot shreds.

Heat oil in a small pan and when hot pour all over the top of fish and listen to the sizzling. Serve at once.

Shredded shallots: Wash shallots and cut into 5 cm lengths. With a sharp knife cut through a few times at one end and put in a bowl of cold water. After 20 minutes, the ends should curl back, so take each one and strip off.

STEAMED WHOLE FISH

1½–2 kg fresh snapper or bream
1 teaspoon salt
1 tablespoon soy sauce
1 teaspoon sugar
2 tablespoons vegetable oil
1 tablespoon sherry
Lengths of shallots or 1 onion

Clean fish, do not remove head, and score. Rub in salt and place on deep plate or casserole ready for steaming.

Mix soy sauce, sugar, oil and sherry together and pour over fish. Sprinkle with cut-up lengths of shallots or onions. Steam for 20 minutes and serve immediately.

If desired, remove fish when cooked and thicken remaining liquor with blended cornflour. Cook for 1 minute over medium heat.

Blended cornflour:

Mix 1 tablespoon cornflour with warm water and 1 teaspoon soy sauce.

WHOLE DEEP-FRIED FISH WITH SWEET AND SOUR SAUCE

1 whole fish approximately
  1–2½ kg
½ teaspoon salt
2 tablespoons cornflour
1 cup oil
1 onion
1 carrot
1 capsicum
1 stick celery

Sauce Ingredients:
½ cup vinegar
2 tablespoons brown sugar
½ teaspoon salt
1 tablespoon tomato sauce
2 tablespoons soy sauce
1 stock cube dissolved in ½
  cup water
½ teaspoon sesame oil
2 tablespoons sweet sherry
2 tablespoons cornflour

Clean fish and split lengthwise through the stomach side to open out flat, being careful not to cut through. Sprinkle with salt and cornflour.

Heat oil in wock or frying pan and, when hot, fry the fish until golden brown, basting constantly. Remove and drain on absorbent paper towel.

Pour off excess oil from the wock and fry the cut-up vegetables until transparent. Stir in the sauce ingredients and cook until thickened.

Place the fish on a serving platter and cover with the sweet and sour sauce.

FISH WITH PINEAPPLE SAUCE

1½ kg fillet of bream or
  flounder
1 teaspoon salt
2 tablespoons soy sauce
1 small can pineapple pieces
2 eggs
3 tablespoons cornflour
Oil for deep-frying

Sauce:
Pineapple juice (from the can
  of pineapple)
Pinch of salt
2 tablespoons cornflour
  blended with 2 tablespoons
  water
1 teaspoon sesame oil

Cut the fillets into chunks approximately 5 cm and place in a bowl. Sprinkle with salt, soy sauce and 2 tablespoons pineapple juice and allow to stand for 10 minutes.

Beat eggs into the cornflour and dip the fish chunks into this batter just before frying.

Heat oil in a deep pan until hot, and deep-fry chunks on both sides until golden brown. Remove and drain.

Put the remainder of the pineapple juice in a small saucepan together with the salt and blended cornflour. Cook until thickened. Then add half of the pineapple pieces to heat through. Just before serving stir in the sesame oil which will give the sauce a glittering translucency.

To serve, place the cooked pieces of fish on a platter, garnish with extra pieces of pineapple and cover with the hot sauce.

FISH CAKES

1 kg fish (white fleshed: pike, teraglin, bream, flathead or jew fish)
1 teaspoon salt
1 teaspoon sugar
2 teaspoons vegetable oil
1 tablespoon cornflour

Mince fish and place in large bowl. Knead gently with salt, sugar and vegetable oil for approximately 10 minutes. Sprinkle with cornflour and continue kneading until mixture is a ball of elasticity.
Shape into 3–4 flat discs. Gently fry on both sides until golden brown, pressing to flatten the cakes as they are cooking. When cool enough to handle, slice into lengths. Serve hot or cold with vegetables.

SLICED FISH CAKES WITH SNOW PEAS

3–4 cooked and sliced fish cakes (see recipe above)
200 g snow peas
2 sticks celery
2 tablespoons vegetable oil
1 clove garlic
1 small onion
½ teaspoon salt
1 teaspoon sugar
1 teaspoon soy sauce
Sherry or wine (optional)
2 tablespoons stock

Remove top and tail from washed snow peas. String celery and cut into 5 cm lengths (see vegetable cutting technique on p. 30).
Have pot of boiling water ready and blanch vegetables for a minute. Remove and drain.
Heat oil in large frying pan and when hot add crushed garlic and onion. When garlic is brown, remove and add snow peas and celery, turning over in the hot oil. Season with salt, sugar, soy sauce and stock. Put in fish cakes and mix well together.
Serve immediately on well-heated shallow dish.

CRAB OMELETTE WITH BROWN SAUCE

1 small can crab
4 eggs
½ teaspoon salt
Oil or butter
¾ cup chicken stock (can use stock cube)
1 tablespoon soy sauce
2 teaspoons cornflour
3 tablespoons cooked green peas

Drain crab, flake and remove fibres. Beat eggs together lightly in a bowl, add salt and mix in the crab meat.
Heat omelette pan or frypan, add oil or butter and when hot, pour in the omelette mixture. Stir the centre of egg mixture gently and cook until centre is almost set. Fold in half and carefully remove to warm serving plate.
Pour stock into small saucepan, mix in soy sauce

(continued)

and cornflour lightly blended with water. Stir gently until sauce boils, then stir in the green peas. Pour sauce over omelette and garnish, if desired, with sprig of parsley or shallot flowers.

BRAISED ABALONE WITH OYSTER SAUCE

1 can abalone
1 cup stock (half abalone liquor and half water)
2 tablespoons cornflour
1 teaspoon soy sauce
1 tablespoon oyster sauce
4 tablespoons brandy
2 slices cooked ham
2 teaspoons oil
Shredded lettuce and Chinese parsley

Drain the liquor from the abalone and slice from side to side into thin pieces.

Put the stock into a small saucepan and bring to the boil.

Blend cornflour with warm water, soy sauce, oyster sauce and brandy. Stir into sauce to cook and thicken.

Mince the cooked ham finely.

Heat wock, add oil and gently turn over the sliced abalone for a few seconds.

Have platter ready with shredded lettuce. Place abalone on top. Cover with the hot sauce and sprinkle with chopped ham. Garnish with Chinese parsley.

CHICKEN AND DUCK

BEGGAR'S CHICKEN
Hart Yee Gai

The one thing that amazes me is that Beggar's Chicken has become a 'glamour' dish. This dish was the discovery of a poor peasant who stole a bird from a poultry farm. He was preparing to cook the chicken using straw and twigs to make a fire. In the middle of his preparation he heard the farmer and his men looking for him. Before he ran away to hide, he took some of the damp clay from the ground, packed it around the chicken and placed it on the remains of the dying fire. In a few hours' time when the peasant returned to retrieve the chicken, he found to his delight upon removing the clay, that the chicken was cooked to a delicious and succulent texture.

Since that time, this technique has been greatly improved, and instead of using moist clay, scone dough or a plain flour dough is used to encase the chicken. There are different variations of the recipe, each chef, no doubt, creating his own interpretation. The cleaned chicken is usually seasoned inside with herbs and spices, covered with a thin sheet of pork fat, wrapped in lotus leaves and encased in dough. It is baked in a slow oven for 2–3 hours, according to size.

Upon service, the whole is brought to the table, flambed with brandy. The dough crust is cut off as a lid, the the lotus leaves peeled aside. The chicken is so tender that it can be easily served with chopsticks or a fork. The natural juices remain inside ensuring a very tender and tasty chicken.

1 fresh chicken, approximately 1½ kg
1 teaspoon salt
2 tablespoons soy sauce
1 teaspoon sesame oil
4 tablespoons brandy (optional)
Slices pork fat
5–6 lotus leaves
Scone dough or plain dough

Clean chicken, wipe dry and rub with salt, soy sauce, sesame oil and brandy.

Cut the pork fat into thin slices and pound them out into thin sheets. Wrap around chicken and parcel the whole with the lotus leaves. (If the lotus leaves are dried, soak in hot water for 15 minutes to soften.)

Encase the whole bird in a scone dough and seal edges securely. Place on a tray and bake in a moderate oven 3–4 hours, turning every 20 minutes while cooking.

To serve, bring to the table flambe, and remove top half of dough as a lid. Unfold lotus leaves and lift out chicken onto a warm serving platter. The

(continued)

chicken will be so tender that the only service required will be chopsticks.

Note: A variation to the recipe is the insertion of minced pork, mushrooms (dried) and strips of shallots in the cavity of the chicken before it is encased in pastry.

CHICKEN AND ALMONDS

1 kg chicken meat
1 teaspoon salt
Pinch bicarbonate of soda
1 egg white
1 teaspoon sesame oil
1 cup vegetable oil
100 g green beans
2 sticks celery
100 g dried mushrooms (or champignons)
10 water chestnuts (or 2 white onions)
Toasted almonds
Parsley

Sauce:
1 cup stock (chicken cube)
1 tablespoon soy sauce
1 tablespoon oyster sauce
2 tablespoons cornflour
3 tablespoons sherry

Cut chicken meat into small dice. Place in a bowl and mix in salt, bicarbonate of soda, egg white, sesame oil.

Heat oil in wock and when hot stir and fry the chicken until it turns colour. Drain.

String green beans and celery and cut into small squares to resemble the size of chicken meat. Plunge into boiling water for 5 minutes. Drain.

Prepare dried mushrooms by soaking for 20 minutes in warm water. Wash, squeeze dry and cut into dice.

Drain liquor from water chestnuts if canned, and cut each chestnut into four parts.

Pour off excess oil in wock, and heat about 1 tablespoon again. Saute all the vegetables together. Return chicken and stock and cook a further few minutes.

Mix sauce ingredients in a bowl and stir into the mixture until thickened. Correct seasoning.

Ladle on to a heated platter, sprinkle with toasted almonds and garnish with a sprig of parsley.

CHICKEN AND WALNUTS

500 g chicken breasts
1 tablespoon cornflour
Salt and pepper
1 tablespoon soy sauce
3 tablespoons sherry
1 tablespoon vegetable oil
Walnuts

Remove skin and bone from chicken breasts. Cut into small dice. Place in a bowl with cornflour, salt, pepper, soy sauce and sherry.

Blanch walnuts and remove skin. Pat dry and fry in hot oil until golden brown. Sprinkle with salt.

Put a little oil in wock and fry the chicken for 5 minutes. Mix in toasted walnuts and serve immediately.

CHICKEN BALLS

500 g chicken meat
2 slices of ham and fat
4 lengths of white ends of shallots
1 teaspoon soy sauce
1 tablespoon sherry
Salt and pepper
1 egg white
Cornflour and fine breadcrumbs (mixed)
Oil for deep-frying

Using two cleavers, chop the chicken and the ham together to make a coarse mince. Place in a bowl. Chop the shallots up finely and stir well into the chicken mixture, together with the seasonings.

Beat the egg white until stiff and fold into the mixture. Keep chilled in the refrigerator for 1 hour.

Shape chicken mixture into small balls with the aid of a spoon and roll lightly in cornflour and breadcrumb mix.

Deep-fry over moderate heat until golden brown. Remove and drain on absorbent paper.

SOY SAUCE CHICKEN

1–1½ kg chicken
Soy Sauce Marinade:
3 litres water
1 length stick cinnamon
4–5 petals star anise (bart gock)
A few cloves
Fennel seeds
Anise herbs
Beetle-nut leaves
Chinese aniseed herbs
1 litre thin soy sauce (sarng chow)
1½ cups black soy sauce (see yo)
½ cup Chinese rock sugar (Bing tong)

Clean and wash chicken. Using tweezers pluck away any tiny feathers that may be left on the skin. Heat a large saucepan with water to cover the chicken and simmer for 20–30 minutes or until just tender. Drain and pat dry.

Boil water with raw spices for one hour, then strain. (Tie the spices in a muslin cloth.) Pour soy sauces into the water and put in the Chinese rock sugar. Suspend the bag of spices in the marinade so that it can be taken out easily.

Bring the soy sauce marinade to the boil and simmer chicken in it for 20–25 minutes. Remove from the heat. Allow chicken to remain in the marinade for another 15 minutes. Remove to warm platter and pour warm vegetable oil over chicken to make it glisten.

When ready to serve, chop up into pieces through the bone, and arrange attractively on platter.

Note: This marinade can be kept indefinitely in the refrigerator to be used for other soy sauce dishes. These include ducks' feet, pigs' trotters, stomach and tripe, giblets, liver, tongues and hard-cooked eggs.

Beggar's Chicken (p. 52) being served.

WHITE WHOLE CHICKEN

1 spring chicken, 1–1½ kg
Soup vegetables
Salt and pepper
2 tablespoons soy sauce
4 tablespoons vegetable oil
1 teaspoon sesame oil

Ginger Sauce:
1 large piece young green ginger
½ teaspoon salt
½ cup vegetable oil
1 teaspoon sesame oil

Bring a large pot of water to the boil with onion and cut-up vegetables.
When the water has come to boiling point, plunge in the cleaned chicken and bring to the boil again. Simmer for 20 minutes. Turn off heat completely and allow the chicken to cook in the heat of the water for approximately another 30 minutes. Remove.
Sprinkle the chicken with fine salt. Spoon over the soy sauce, vegetables oils.
Allow to cool, and serve cold with salads or use chicken meat for noodle dishes.
If serving hot, chop chicken with bone attached and serve with ginger sauce.
Scrape skin from ginger, cut into pieces and mince finely with cleaver. Place in a small bowl. Mix in salt. Heat oils and when hot, pour into minced ginger.

Note: Keep chicken stock and use for sauces and soup.

CURRIED CHICKEN MALAYSIAN

1 chicken
2 tablespoons vegetable oil
6 cloves garlic (shallot bulbs if obtainable)
2–3 tablespoons curry powder
1 tablespoon curry paste (or ½ teaspoon five spice)
1 litre stock
1 large onion
3–4 potatoes
1 tablespoon coconut cream

Wash and clean chicken, then chop through the bone, into large pieces.
Heat oil in frying pan, fry garlic cloves until brown, then put in chicken and fry for 5 minutes.
Put in curry powder, curry paste and cook a further 2–3 minutes to bring out flavour of the curry powder. Season with salt and pepper.
Pour over the stock, add diced onion and potato and cook until chicken and potatoes are tender, approximately 30 minutes.
Heat the coconut cream in the curry sauce until thickened and simmer a further 10 minutes.
Keep curry in an earthenware pot and keep at least overnight before reheating to use. It is generally better if kept for a longer period, say about one week.
Serve with steamed rice.

Top: Walnut Chicken Bonbon (p. 61) Bottom: Whole Chicken in Pineapple Sauce (p. 57).

SLICED CHICKEN WITH BEAN SPROUTS

1 kg young chicken
1 tablespoon soy sauce
3 tablespoons whisky
½ teaspoon salt
1 clove garlic
1 egg white
200 g bean sprouts
1 green capsicum
Oil for deep-frying
Seasoning Sauce:
2 tablespoons stock
1 tablespoon vinegar
2 teaspoons sugar
1 teaspoon sesame oil
1 tablespoon soy sauce
1 tablespoon cornflour

Fillet chicken and cut into 4 cm slices. Marinate in soy sauce, whisky, salt and crushed garlic. Stir in the egg white.
Cut ends from bean sprouts and wash thoroughly. Parboil in boiling water for 2–3 minutes. Remove and drain.
Cut capsicum into lengths.
Deep-fry chicken for 1 minute and remove. Pour off most of the excess oil and saute bean sprouts and capsicum.
Return chicken and stir-fry constantly.
Add the seasoning sauce and stir until thickened. Serve immediately.

CHICKEN BEAN SAUCE WITH GINGER

2 chicken breasts
Salt and pepper
1 teaspoon cornflour
1 egg white
150 g green beans
1 onion
1 stick celery
2 cm piece green ginger
2 tablespoons black beans
1 tablespoon brandy
½ teaspoon sugar
2 tablespoons vegetable oil
1 tablespoon cornflour
2 tablespoons water or stock

Remove bone and skin from chicken breast. Flatten with meat cleaver and cut chicken into thin slices. Sprinkle with salt, pepper and cornflour and mix in egg white.
String beans and slice into 5 cm diagonal lengths. Blanch for 5 minutes, drain.
Slice onion and celery into lengths. Scrape skin from green ginger and shred finely.
Wash black beans, squeeze dry and chop finely with knife. Put into a bowl, with brandy, sugar and shredded ginger.
Heat vegetable oil in a frying pan or wock and fry chicken until tender. Remove to platter. Fry onion, celery and beans, pour in black bean sauce. Return chicken to mixture and combine well together. Cook in the blended cornflour.
Serve on heated platter garnished with Chinese parsley.

WHOLE CHICKEN IN PINEAPPLE SAUCE

1½–2 kg whole chicken
½ cup thin soy sauce
1 teaspoon salt
4 tablespoons brandy
Oil for deep-frying
1 small can pineapple pieces
1 onion
2 cups water
½ cup raisins
1 tablespoon cornflour

Marinate chicken in combined soy sauce, salt and brandy for 1 hour, turning over once or twice. Drain well and reserve marinade. Pat dry chicken with absorbent paper towel. Deep-fry chicken in hot oil until golden brown. Remove from pan.
Drain pineapple and reserve ½ cup of the syrup. Fry chopped onion until transparent, pour in the reserved marinade, pineapple syrup and water. Add chicken, cover and simmer until tender.
Remove chicken to serving dish. Put the pineapple pieces and raisins in the sauce and cook in the blended cornflour until thickened.
Spoon the sauce over the chicken and decorate with extra pineapple and raisins.

CRISP SKIN CHICKEN

1½–2 kg whole fresh chicken
1 teaspoon salt
1 piece star anise
Peppercorns
Cut-up vegetables (carrot, onion, celery)
Cornflour
Oil for deep-frying

Basting Sauce:
2 tablespoons honey
1 tablespoon vinegar
2 tablespoons warm water
2 tablespoons rose wine or sherry
Salt and pepper

Place cleaned chicken in a large saucepan of boiling water, to which salt, star anise, peppercorns and cut-up vegetables have already been added. Bring to the boil and then simmer for 20 minutes. Remove the chicken when cool and pat dry.
Tie a string around the chicken's neck and place in a shallow bowl with basting sauce. Turn frequently. Leave to marinate about 1 hour, or until there is no more sauce left. Sprinkle bird generously with cornflour. Hang the chicken by the string in a cool place to dry thoroughly, overnight preferably.
Deep-fry chicken over moderate heat, basting all the while so that it will turn an even golden brown colour. Use the string as a lever for manipulating the bird. During the final stages of cooking, lower the whole bird into the deep oil to ensure that it is completely cooked. Remove and drain on absorbent paper towels.
To serve, the chicken is chopped through the bone and garnished with lemon wedges. It is eaten with fried salt and pepper or peppercorn salt. (see p. 61).

CHICKEN PIECES WITH LEMON SAUCE

10 chicken pieces
1 teaspoon salt
2 tablespoons vegetable oil
  (or substitute lard)

Lemon Sauce:
½ cup bottled lemon sauce
2 tablespoons sweet sherry
½ cup water

Put chicken pieces in baking dish. Sprinkle with salt and spoon over with vegetable oil. Cook in moderate oven until tender, approximately 1 hour. Remove to serving dish.

Put lemon sauce in a small saucepan. Add sherry and enough water to mix into a pouring consistency. Stir until boiling. Spoon over the chicken pieces.

STEAMED CHICKEN WITH SALAMI

1 kg spring chicken
1 teaspoon salt
1 tablespoon cornflour
1 teaspoon soy sauce
1 tablespoon peanut oil
½ teaspoon sesame oil
3 tablespoons rose wine
1 pair Chinese salami (larp cheong)
2 dried mushrooms, soaked and washed
Shallots

Cut chicken up into pieces and sprinkle with salt and cornflour. Place in a shallow casserole ready for steaming.

In a small bowl, mix together the soy sauce, vegetable oils and rose wine. Pour over the chicken.

Wipe the salami with a warm cloth and cut into slices on the bias. Place over the top of chicken in casserole. Slice prepared mushrooms and sprinkle on top.

Steam for approximately 30 minutes. Serve with a garnish of shallot flowers.

CHICKEN ROLLS

1 kg whole chicken
6 dehydrated mushrooms
10 fresh water chestnuts or 1 piece of bamboo shoot
Salt and pepper
2 tablespoons soy sauce
3 tablespoons sherry
½ teaspoon five spice
2 eggs (yolks are used to brush on finished roll)
Pork caul (mung yo)
Cornflour
Oil for deep-frying

Fillet the chicken and separate the white meat from the dark. Flatten the white meat with a mallet and cut the dark meat into lengths.

Soak mushrooms for 20 minutes in warm water, then wash and squeeze dry. Cut into lengths. Peel chestnuts if fresh, and cut into lengths also. If using bamboo shoots, cut into lengths resembling the mushrooms.

In a large flat dish put in the chicken meat, salt and pepper, soy sauce, sherry and five spice. Pour over egg white and allow to marinate for 30 minutes at least.

(continued)

Wash pork caul thoroughly, being careful not to tear it as it is very fine. Cut into large lengths the same size as the white chicken meat.

Lay the pork caul on a flat surface and place the white chicken meat on top. Alternately put in a length of dark chicken meat, mushroom, bamboo shoot or chestnuts, and roll up tightly to resemble the size of a small jam roll. Place in refrigerator for 1 hour to set.

When ready for deep-frying, brush with beaten egg yolk and sprinkle with cornflour. Deep-fry until golden brown over moderate heat. Drain on absorbent paper.

Cut into sections when serving. Eat hot or cold.

Note: Pork caul (mung yo) can be purchased at the larger Chinese delicatessens in large cities. It is the lining of the pig's stomach, very very fine, resembling a net. It has to be handled gently or its threads will break.

ROAST CHICKEN SATE

1 chicken up to 1 kg in weight
1 teaspoon salt
1 teaspoon coriander seeds
2 tablespoons raw peanuts
2 red hot chilis
1 teaspoon five spice powder
1 teaspoon curry powder
$\frac{1}{2}$ teaspoon turmeric
$\frac{1}{2}$ teaspoon sugar
1 cup coconut milk
1 teaspoon lemon juice
3 tablespoons vegetable oil
1 tablespoon toasted coconut

Prepare chicken and sprinkle with salt, inside and outside.

Pound coriander, peanuts and red chilis together. Mix in five spice, curry powder, turmeric and sugar. Fry these ingredients in a little oil for 3–4 minutes until all the flavours are released. Do not burn. Remove from pan and cool. Rub over chicken, inside and outside.

Place chicken in a roasting pan. Pour over the coconut milk, vegetable oil and lemon juice. Cook in a moderate oven for approximately 1 hour or until brown and tender.

Serve cut-up chicken with the gravy juices over top and sprinkle with toasted coconut.

Note: This roast chicken is Malayan style and if you do not want to go to the trouble of making the sate ingredients, use the bottled variety. There is no substitute for the fragrant aroma of the spices cooking.

COLD CHICKEN AND SEAWEED SALAD

100 g agar-agar (see glossary) or substitute very fine vermicelli
½ cup celery, cut into matchstick size
1 green cucumber, cut into matchstick size
1 large slice ham, shredded
1 cup shredded cooked chicken

Sesame Paste Dressing:
2 tablespoons sesame paste (substitute peanut butter)
1 tablespoon soy sauce
2 tablespoons white vinegar
1 teaspoon sugar
1 tablespoon sesame oil
1 teaspoon mustard
½ cup salad oil

Cut agar-agar into 5 cm pieces with scissors. Soak in warm water for 20 minutes and squeeze dry by patting method between two sheets of absorbent towels. Place on serving platter.
Arrange the celery and cucumber on top of agar-agar. Arrange ham and chicken on top. Keep cool in refrigerator.
Serve with home-made sate sauce (p. 42) or sesame paste dressing.

Mix all the ingredients in a small bowl and serve over the chicken salad.

Note: If using vermicelli, cook as directed and allow to cool first.

CHICKEN AND PORK WITH VEGETABLES

200 g cooked chicken and pork
100 g cellophane noodles
1 piece of bamboo shoot
1 stalk celery
1 tablespoon fungi (chee yue)
½ cup stock
1 tablespoon soy sauce
½ teaspoon salt

Cut cooked chicken and pork into matchstick size. Soak noodles in warm water for 10 minutes until limp. Drain.
Cut bamboo shoot into matchstick size. Peel fibres from celery and cut into same size. Plunge celery in boiling water for 5 minutes. Remove and drain. Soak fungi in warm water for 10 minutes. Wash and squeeze dry.
Heat oil in wock and when hot, saute celery, fungi and bamboo shoot. Add stock, salt and soy sauce. Put in cooked chicken and pork and cellophane noodles. Mix thoroughly and stir-fry for 5 minutes. Adjust seasoning.
Serve hot.

WALNUT CHICKEN BONBON

2 whole chicken breasts
½ teaspoon salt
2 tablespoons cornflour
2 egg whites
1 cup walnuts
Oil for deep-frying

Remove chicken meat from bones and discard skin. Flatten gently with a meat cleaver. Slice chicken into 5 cm lengths. Sprinkle with salt and cornflour. Dip into egg white. Allow to stand at least 20 minutes, so that the chicken is moist all over.

Put walnuts in a saucepan of boiling water and boil 2 or 3 minutes. Leave the nuts in the water and, when cool enough to handle, remove the brown skin. This is a tedious job but well worth the time involved for the success of the dish. Use a blender or chop the nuts finely.

Roll the chicken in the chopped walnuts, patting them firmly to form a tight cover. Deep-fry in hot oil until golden brown. Serve with fried salt and pepper or peppercorn salt.

Fried Salt and Pepper:
1 teaspoon salt
1 teaspoon ground pepper
2 teaspoons five spice powder

Mix spices in a small shallow pan. Stir gently over low heat for 2 minutes. The cooking of the spices releases the flavours.

Peppercorn Salt:
2 tablespoons black peppercorns
2 tablespoons salt

Mix the peppercorns and salt together in a dry frying pan and stir for approximately 1 minute. When salt turns a golden brown remove from heat. Allow to cool. Grind until very fine; if necessary sift with a fine sieve. Store in an airtight container.

EASY PEKING DUCK

1 fat duck
1 teaspoon salt
1 length shallot
3 tablespoons vegetable oil
½ cup barbecue sauce (hoi sin jeung)
Pancakes
Shallot flowers

Wash and clean duck thoroughly plucking out the minute feathers on the skin. Remove the oil sacs from the tail of the duck.

With a straw, blow air between the breast and skin of duck which will separate the fatty part from the skin. Sprinkle inside and outside with salt. Place a piece of shallot inside duck.

Place duck on a roasting pan with the oil and cook in slow heat for 1 hour.

Brush the barbecue sauce over duck and cook for a further 20 minutes. Brush again with barbecue sauce and continue cooking until duck is crisp and brown.

To serve, take the skin off and cut into 5 cm squares. Slice the meat the same way and put on separate platter.

Have prepared steamed bread buns or pancakes. Spread hoisin sauce on the bread or pancake, roll a piece of duck, skin and strips of shallot inside and eat like a sandwich.

MEATS

HOT RICE STEAK

500 g topside or rump steak
1 cup raw rice
½ teaspoon five spice
Lettuce

Seasonings:
2 tablespoons soy sauce
2 petals star anise
½ teaspoon sugar
1 teaspoon salt and pepper
1 tablespoon sate sauce (any hot bean sauce)
2 tablespoons vegetable oil

Cut the beef into dice approximately 4 cm × 4 cm and ½ cm thick. Marinate in the seasonings for 30 minutes.

Fry rice in a dry frying pan with five spice until brown. Remove to a flat surface and when cool, put in blender and reduce to size of fine bread-crumbs.

Dip beef into rice crumbs and place on a shallow plate ready for steaming. Steam for approximately 20 minutes and serve over shredded lettuce.

SATE BEEF WITH CAULIFLOWER

500 g sirloin of beef
1 tablespoon soy sauce
1 tablespoon vegetable oil
1 teaspoon sesame oil
Salt and pepper
2 cm green ginger
2 cups cauliflower
½ cup water
1 capsicum
3 tablespoons oil
1 tablespoon sate sauce
1 tablespoon cornflour blended with 1 tablespoon water

Cut meat into 4 cm slices. Place on a flat plate and sprinkle with soy sauce, vegetable oil, salt and pepper. Shred green ginger finely and place next to beef.

Break cauliflower into flowerets and slice the stalks into thin pieces. Put into saucepan with the water and boil for 5 minutes. Remove and drain. Cut-up capsicum.

Heat oil in wock and fry the beef until brown, adding a little at a time. Add ginger and veg-etables. Stir-fry for 5 minutes.

Mix sate sauce with the liquor left over from cauliflower and the blended cornflour. Add to mixture and cook approximately 3–4 minutes. Serve on heated platter. This dish is at its best when eaten immediately.

DEEP-FRIED BEEF WITH CAULIFLOWER

250 g fillet of beef
Piece of cauliflower
1 piece of bamboo shoot (or substitute white onion)
10 water chestnuts (or substitute celery)
Oil for deep-frying

Sauce:
½ cup stock
Salt and pepper
1 tablespoon soy sauce
1 tablespoon oyster sauce
1 tablespoon tomato sauce
1 tablespoon blended cornflour
½ teaspoon sesame oil

Slice beef into lengths of 5 cm strips, across the grain.

Break cauliflower into flowerets, peel stalks of fibre and cut into thin slices. Cook in a little water for 5 minutes. Drain. Cut bamboo shoot and water chestnuts into strips.

Heat oil in wock and deep-fry the cauliflower first. Remove, then replenish oil, if necessary, and deep-fry the meat. This will only take 4–5 minutes. Remove and pour off excess oil.

Saute bamboo shoot and water chestnuts for 2 minutes, then pour in the sauce ingredients and cook until thickened.

Gently mix in the beef and cauliflower to heat through. Serve immediately.

SLICED BEEF WITH OYSTER SAUCE

500 g topside or fillet steak
2 tablespoons vegetable oil
1 teaspoon sesame oil
1 clove garlic
1 piece fresh green ginger
1 egg white
Oil for deep-frying
1 small white onion
3 tablespoons oyster sauce (hor yo)
1 tablespoon stock or water
1 sweet red pepper

Slice beef diagonally into lengths approximately 5 cm × 1 cm. Marinate meat in vegetable oils, crushed ginger and garlic, and egg white for 30 minutes.

Heat oil and deep-fry meat until nicely browned. Remove to warm platter. Pour off excess oil in pan and fry onion until transparent.

Mix oyster sauce with stock in a small bowl.

Return meat to onion in pan and pour in oyster sauce. Continue to stir and cook for 5 minutes.

Serve hot with steamed white rice. Decorate with red pepper.

WHOLE FILLET OF BEEF WITH BLACK BEAN SAUCE

900 g fillet of beef or scotch steak in one piece
1 tablespoon vegetable oil
Pepper

Wrap fillet of beef in aluminium foil leaving top free. Place in baking dish. Spoon oil over top and sprinkle with pepper. Bake in moderate oven allowing 20 minutes per 500 g of beef. *(continued)*

Black Bean Sauce:
4 tablespoons black beans
2 tablespoons rose wine or sweet sherry
Shredded green ginger
1 beef stock cube
2 tablespoons cornflour blended in 1 cup water

Wash black beans thoroughly. Chop into tiny pieces. Place black beans in baking dish or small saucepan and pour in any liquor from the fillet of beef. Add crumbled stock cube, shredded ginger and blended cornflour. Bring to the boil stirring all the time and cook for 2 minutes. Add wine.

When beef is done, cut into thick slices and pour black bean sauce over each serving.

SPARE RIBS WITH GARLIC SAUCE

2 kg beef spare ribs
5–6 cloves garlic
1 piece fresh green ginger
3 teaspoons five spice powder
3 tablespoons rose wine or sherry
2 teaspoons salt
1 teaspoon sugar
½ cup vegetable oil

Chop spare ribs into 5 cm lengths and place in a deep bowl. Mince garlic and ginger. Add to spare ribs. Sprinkle with the five spice powder. Add the rose wine, salt, sugar and vegetable oil. Mix ingredients well together and allow to marinate for at least 1 hour or, even better, overnight.

Bake on aluminium foil in hot oven for 15 minutes, basting several times. Reduce heat and finish cooking, allowing about another 15 minutes.

SATE BEEF FLAMBE

1 small fillet of beef
1 teaspoon salt
1 tablespoon soy sauce
1 piece green ginger
2 cloves garlic
2 tablespoons vegetable oil
1 teaspoon sesame oil
½ teaspoon sugar
2 onions
Sauce:
2 tablespoons sate sauce (purchased in jars)
1 teaspoon oyster sauce
¼ cup stock (stock cube)
1 teaspoon tabasco (or less)

Cut fillet of beef into thin roundels. Place in a bowl with salt, soy sauce, crushed ginger and garlic, vegetable oils and sugar. Allow to marinate for 30 minutes.

Peel and slice onions in fine shreds. Sprinkle all round oyster platter.

Heat a little oil in wock and saute the beef for 2–3 minutes or as long as 5 minutes if preferred. Discard the ginger and garlic.

Stir in sauce ingredients and cook for 2 minutes over moderate heat, then cover with a lid and simmer for 2–3 minutes more.

Take wock and contents off heat, flambe with warm brandy.

Place beef on top of onion shreds. Garnish with a sprig of parsley. Ignite the lemon essence over cube of sugar in centre cup of oyster platter and serve immediately.

BRAISED SKIRT STEAK

Kno Bark Narm

1 kg skirt steak (with sinew)
2 teaspoons salt
3 tablespoons soy sauce
1 teaspoon brown sugar
3 tablespoons rose wine (or sherry)
2 cloves garlic
4 tablespoons vegetable oil
2 cups stock (use beef cube)
4–5 petals Chinese aniseed (bart gock)
½ teaspoon five spice powder
Shallot flowers

Cut skirt steak into approximately 5 cm × 2 cm pieces. Marinate for 30 minutes with salt, soy sauce, brown sugar, rose wine, crushed garlic and 1 tablespoon vegetable oil.

Heat wock or deep frying pan with the other 3 tablespoons of vegetable oil and fry steak until it browns evenly.

Pour in stock, add Chinese aniseed and five spice powder and allow to simmer until meat is tender, approximately 30 minutes.

Remove petals of Chinese aniseed and garlic. Decorate with shallot flowers. There should be just enough sauce to keep meat succulent.

Note: This dish also can be used as a topping over rice noodles.

MOTHER'S FAVOURITE POTATO BALLS

Mashed potatoes
Flour (1 part flour to 3 parts mashed potato)
Cornflour for dusting

Meat Filling:
500 g minced steak
2–3 rashers bacon
1 onion
Salt and pepper
½ teaspoon curry powder
3 tablespoons cooked green peas
1 tablespoon hoisin sauce
2 tablespoons oil

Place warm mashed potato into a bowl. Sift in the flour and knead into a firm dough. Pull off about 6 cm piece of dough and flatten into a circle on the palm of the hand.

For filling, place minced steak in a bowl. Cut bacon and onion into small dice and mix into steak. Season with salt, pepper, curry powder and add the green peas and hoisin sauce.

Heat oil in wock and gently fry the seasoned steak for approximately 5 minutes.

Spoon filling in centre of a circle of dough and close to make a ball. Continue until all dough and filling are used. Refrigerate for 1 hour.

Roll potato balls lightly in cornflour and deep-fry over moderate heat until golden brown.

Serve either hot or cold.

SHIN OF BEEF WITH VEGETABLES

800 g shin of beef
2 tablespoons oil or lard
500 g potatoes, parsnips or turnips
2 cloves garlic
2 teaspoons red bean curd
1 teaspoon sugar
1 teaspoon salt
1 tablespoon sherry
Water or stock

Cut meat into 3 cm dice and fry in oil or lard with the crushed garlic, until meat turns colour, using a deep saucepan.

Cover with water or stock and cook until almost tender, approximately 1 hour. Mash red bean curd and add to beef together with seasonings.

Cut up vegetables into same size as beef. If potatoes are included, use new potatoes of uniform size. Add vegetables to saucepan and finish cooking until all are tender. Thicken the gravy with blended cornflour, if desired.

Serve in a deep bowl or tureen and garnish with Chinese parsley. This dish can be cooked ahead of time and placed in a casserole to be heated in the oven when desired.

BRAISED BEEF WITH TOMATOES

250 g sirloin of beef
Salt and pepper
½ teaspoon sugar
2 cloves garlic
2 tablespoons vegetable oil
1 teaspoon cornflour
3–4 tomatoes
2 onions
1 teaspoon tomato paste
Sauce:
1 tablespoon cornflour
3 tablespoons stock
1 tablespoon soy sauce
1 teaspoon oyster sauce

Slice beef into lengths of 5 cm. Mix with salt, pepper, sugar, crushed garlic and vegetable oil. Sprinkle with cornflour.

Cut tomato and onion into wedges.

Put oil in wock and swirl around until hot. Saute beef for 3 minutes. Remove to platter.

Put in onion and fry until transparent, then add tomatoes and tomato paste.

Return beef to mixture and pour in the blended cornflour, stock, soy sauce and oyster sauce. Cook until thickened. Cover with a lid and braise for 5 minutes.

Serve hot with steamed white rice.

BRANDIED ROAST PORK

2 kg pork loin
2 tablespoons salt
1 teaspoon raw sugar
1–2 teaspoons five spice
2–3 tablespoons French brandy

Score skin of pork loin ready for roasting.

Heat wock and fry salt over moderate heat. Remove to small bowl. Mix in the raw sugar, five spice and brandy. Smear this mixture on the inside of the pork loin.

(continued)

Place on rack in a hot oven to roast skin during first 15 minutes of cooking. Reduce heat to moderate and continue cooking until pork is well done, approximately another 1½–2 hours.

To serve, remove crackling, and flambe with brandy. Cut into slices and serve with green vegetable combination.

Note: This is a favourite recipe learnt from my Cordon Bleu Chinese teacher from Shanghai.

MINCE CURRY IN A HURRY

250 g minced steak
2 onions
2 tablespoons vegetable oil
2–3 tablespoons curry powder
Salt and pepper
1–2 tomatoes
3 tablespoons frozen green peas
1 beef stock cube
1 cup water
1 tablespoon soy sauce
1 teaspoon sesame oil (optional)
1 teaspoon dried coriander (optional)

Cut onion into small dice. Heat oil in wock or frying pan and fry onion until transparent. Put in the curry powder and fry for 1 minute.

Add the minced steak, salt and pepper and stir-fry until the meat changes colour. Cut tomatoes into quarters and add to mince. Put in the frozen green peas. Remove the skin from tomatoes, which will come away with the heat in cooking.

Sprinkle in the beef stock, add water, soy sauce, sesame oil and coriander. Continue to simmer for 25–30 minutes, Correct seasoning.

Serve with hot cooked rice.

BEEF AND TOMATO MOULD

500 g beef steak
Salt and pepper
1 tablespoon soy sauce
1 tablespoon salad oil
1 teaspoon sesame oil
1 teaspoon cornflour
4 tomatoes
1 teaspoon sugar
1 piece green ginger
Shallots

Slice beef across the grain into 5 cm strips. Place in a bowl, season with salt and pepper. Using chopsticks or a fork, stir in soy sauce, vegetable oils and cornflour.

Cut tomatoes into quarters and sprinkle with sugar. Place four quarters of a tomato in the centre of the beef and put the other tomatoes on top.

Sprinkle with shredded ginger and chopped shallots and steam for 20 minutes.

(continued)

Note. This is a family favourite and the cheaper cuts of meat are ideal for this recipe. Try it when tomatoes are cheap. This dish is better when left overnight, and steamed for 10 minutes the next day. Sometimes I vary it with a capsicum.

ROAST PORK WITH PLUM SAUCE

800 g lean pork fillets
½ cup soy sauce
2 tablespoons red wine
1 tablespoon brown sugar
2 tablespoons vegetable oil
½ teaspoon red food colouring
1 clove garlic
½ teaspoon cinnamon
1 length of shallot
1 teaspoon salt

Combine soy sauce, red wine, brown sugar, vegetable oil and colouring in a bowl. Add crushed garlic and cut-up lengths of shallot.
Sprinkle cinnamon and salt on pork fillets. Marinate pork fillets at least 1 hour or refrigerate overnight, turning occasionally.
Drain from marinade, put on rack in baking dish and bake in moderate oven turning frequently with tongs and basting with drippings from pork. Cut into thin slices and serve with a small dish of plum sauce.

Note: Five spice powder can be substituted for cinnamon. This will impart a stonger flavour.

ROAST BELLY PORK

1½–2 kg belly pork
Seasonings:
1 teaspoon salt
2 tablespoons sweet bean sauce
1 teaspoon five spice
1 tablespoon soy sauce

Score the skin of pork into long strips about 2 cm wide.
Mix seasonings in a bowl into a stiff paste. Rub this mixture on the bottom of the pork, *not* the top.
Place on a rack over a shallow baking dish with a little water at the bottom and roast with highest heat for the first 15 minutes. This will crisp the skin to make a beautiful crackling. Continue to cook with moderate heat for another 40 minutes or until pork is well done.
When pork is cool cut off crackling and slice.
Serve with hot vegetables or fried rice.

SWEET AND SOUR PORK

1 kg belly pork
1 teaspoon salt
1 egg
1 tablespoon cornflour
3 tablespoons flour
3–4 tablespoons water
Oil for deep-frying

Sauce:
1 onion
1 capsicum
1 cup pineapple pieces
2 tablespoons cornflour
   blended with ½ cup water
   or stock
1 tablespoon wine vinegar
2 tablespoons sugar
1 teaspoon soy sauce
1 teaspoon tomato sauce
⅓ cup pineapple juice
¼ teaspoon salt
½ teaspoon sesame oil

Remove the rind from pork. Cut the pork into 2 cm squares. Sprinkle with salt.

Beat the egg, and mix into cornflour and flour with enough water to make a thick batter. Stir the pork into the batter to cover evenly.

Heat the oil and deep-fry pork squares, adding a few at a time, until golden brown. Remove. Drain on absorbent paper. Just before serving, deep-fry again for a couple of minutes.

For the sauce, fry the cut-up onion in a small saucepan until transparent (do not brown). Add the diced capsicum and pineapple. Pour in the rest of the sauce ingredients and stir over slow heat until thickened.

Pour the sauce over the pork and decorate with extra pieces of pineapple.

BARBECUED PORK

1½ –2kg pork fillets or pork
   loin
3–4 cloves garlic
4–6 shallot bulbs
3 tablespoons barbecue sauce
2 tablespoons sesame paste
   (or peanut butter)
2 tablespoons sweet soy bean
   paste
2 teaspoons five spice powder
1 tablespoon salt
1 teaspoon sugar
4–6 tablespoons soy sauce
½ cup vegetable or salad oil
4 tablespoons brandy
Few drops red vegetable
colouring

If using pork loin, debone and cut into lengths to resemble pork fillets.

Chop the garlic and shallot bulbs up very finely and put in a large bowl with all the seasonings, brandy and red colouring. Mix well together. Marinate the pork for approximately 1 hour, or better, overnight.

Using a long skewer, secure pork tightly and barbecue over the coals. If using oven, prepare a wire rack over a tray to catch the drippings, and allow approximately 20 minutes to each kilo of pork.

Note: Chinese chefs skewer the pieces of pork lengthwise using a clothes-hanger type of rod with a cover and cook them in a deep oven.

Barbecued pork (above).

STIR FRIED PORK WITH STRING BEANS

500 g pork
1 tablespoon soy sauce
3 tablespoons vegetable oil
1 piece fresh green ginger
1 clove garlic
Salt and pepper
150 g fresh string beans
1 large onion
1 tablespoon sweet bean paste
(substitute soy or barbecue
sauce)
1 tablespoon cornflour

Cut the pork into 5 cm × 1 cm lengths approximately. Marinate for 10 minutes, with the soy sauce, vegetable oil, shredded ginger, crushed garlic and salt.

String beans and cut into lengths approximately the size of pork. Parboil for 3–4 minutes and remove. Reserve liquor for stock.

Slice onion from top to bottom and fry in a little oil for 1 minute. Remove to platter. Add a little more oil to the wock and fry the pork briskly until it is well seared. Return onion and stir in the string beans.

Mix sweet bean paste with stock in a bowl and blend in the cornflour. Add to the pork and vegetable mixture and cook until the sauce is thickened. Adjust seasoning and serve immediately. Remove garlic if preferred.

STEAMED PORK BUNS

Dough:
500 g flour
1 tablespoon dried yeast
1 tablespoon sugar
1½ cups warm water (approximately)
1 tablespoon milk

Filling: (for 12 buns)
250 g barbecued pork (see recipe p. 70)
Chopped white ends of shallots
6 dried mushrooms
1 tablespoon hoisin sauce

Sift flour into a bowl. Sprinkle yeast in another basin with the sugar and milk. Mix and allow to ferment about 15 minutes. Use water and yeast to make into a bread-like dough. Allow to stand and prove. Knead again and make into a long sausage roll. (A package of yeast dough may be used instead if available.)

Soak and wash mushrooms and boil for 20 minutes. Cut pork into small dice. Also cut mushrooms into same size. Combine in a bowl with the shallots. Stir in hoisin sauce and mix well together. Slice dough roll into 6 cm pieces. Flatten into a circle and put filling into centre. Close at the top by giving a little twist and take off excess dough. Have some small squares of greaseproof paper ready and place the buns on top.

Allow to stand for 10 minutes before steaming. Steam for 15–20 minutes.
Serve either hot or cold.

Stir-fried Pork with String Beans (above).

RED ROAST SPARE RIBS

1 kg pork spare ribs
3 tablespoons soy sauce
2–3 tablespoons red bean curd
   (narm ya)
1 tablespoon sesame paste (or
   peanut paste)
1 teaspoon salt
1 piece fresh green ginger
2 cloves garlic
3 tablespoons rose wine (mui
   gway lo)
1 tablespoon honey, diluted
   in warm water
½ cup vegetable oil

Chop spare ribs into approximately 5 cm lengths and place in a deep bowl.

Mix together in another small bowl, placed over hot water, the soy sauce, mashed red bean curd, sesame paste, salt, crushed ginger, garlic, rose wine, honey and oil. Pour over the spare ribs and allow to marinate at least 1 hour, or place in the refrigerator overnight.

Prepare spare ribs for cooking on a flat tray, preferably lined with aluminium foil to catch the drippings, and cook in a hot oven for 20–30 minutes Baste with the pan drippings. Turn heat down and cook a further 25 minutes or until the ribs are cooked.

Note: For a barbecue, leave the ribs whole and cook over the hot coals.

BRAISED PORK ROLLS

12 slices of lean pork cut wafer
   thin
3–4 dehydrated mushrooms
1 piece of bamboo shoot
Shallots
2 tablespoons oil
Sauce:
½ cup stock
1 tablespoon soy sauce
1 teaspoon salt
2 tablespoons vinegar
1 tablespoon sugar (to taste)
1 tablespoon vegetable oil
1 teaspoon sesame oil

Pound the pork to make even a finer sheet.

Soak mushrooms in warm water for 20 minutes and then wash and squeeze dry. Cut into matchstick size.

Cut the bamboo shoot into same size. Dip the shallots into hot water for 5 minutes and then strip into long lengths.

Place one length of mushroom and bamboo shoot on the sheet of pork and roll up firmly. Fasten with a tooth pick or tie with length of shallot.

Heat oil in wock and put in the pork rolls to brown evenly, approximately 2 minutes. Remove.

Place pork rolls on a shallow casserole, pour over the sauce amd steam for 25–30 minutes.

To serve, arrange the pork rolls on a warm platter and cover with the sauce. If desired, thicken the sauce with a little cornflour.

STEAMED SPARERIBS WITH BLACK BEAN SAUCE

500 g pork or beef spareribs
3 tablespoons black beans (dow see)
1 slice green ginger
3 tablespoons soy sauce
½ teaspoon sugar
3 tablespoons rose wine or sherry
2 teaspoons oyster sauce
Salt and pepper
2 tablespoons water
1 tablespoon vegetable oil
Chopped shallots or 1 small white onion for garnish

Chop spareribs into 3 cm sections and place in a large bowl.
Wash black beans, squeeze dry and chop finely. Mix into spareribs together with shredded ginger and seasonings. Allow to marinate for 30 minutes. Place the spareribs on a shallow casserole and prepare for steaming. Steam for 30 minutes. Garnish with finely chopped shallots or onion.
Serve with hot steaming white rice.

SPRING ROLLS

100 g roast pork
100 g cooked shrimps
250 g bean sprouts or shredded cabbage
6 dried mushrooms (soaked for 20 minutes)
2 slices ham fat
Noodle pastry wrappers approximately 14 cm

Cut roast pork and shrimps into matchstick shapes.
If using bean sprouts, cut off both ends and wash thoroughly, blanch and drain. Shred cabbage, wash and drain. Shred mushrooms and ham fat.
Place 2 tablespoons of filling on spring roll wrappers and enclose securely, tucking in both sides as if wrapping a parcel.
Place on shallow casserole and steam for 10 minutes. Allow to cool and pat dry.
Heat oil in a deep saucepan and gently slide in the spring rolls to deep-fry until golden brown.
Serve either hot or cold with extra soy sauce and/or tabasco chili sauce.
If serving as an entree, serve spring rolls with finely chopped almonds on top.

BARBECUED SAVOURY SPARE RIBS

1 kg pork spare ribs

Seasoning:
4 tablespoons soy sauce
1 teaspoon salt
1 tablespoon honey
1 tablespoon sweet bean paste
2 cloves garlic
1 piece sliced green ginger
½ teaspoon five spice (heong liu fun)
3 tablespoons vegetable oil
½ cup whisky
1 tablespoon sesame paste

Marinate spare ribs in a deep bowl with all the seasonings. If left overnight in the refrigerator the spare ribs will be more flavoursome.

Cook over barbecue or in a hot oven until brown and thoroughly cooked. Chop into small pieces if too large.

Serve with sweet and sour sauce or plum sauce dip.

PINEAPPLE SPARE RIBS

2 kg spare ribs

Sauce:
1 small can crushed pineapple
2 tablespoons soy sauce
4 tablespoons salad oil
2 tablespoons sweet bean paste (hoisin jeung) (or use 2 tablespoons honey dilluted in warm water)
1 piece of crushed ginger and garlic
4 tablespoons tomato sauce
Lemon juice
Salt and pepper

Chop up spare ribs into 5 cm lengths. Place into a large saucepan with enough water to cover. Boil for 10 minutes. Remove and drain.

Mix the sauce ingredients together in a deep bowl and marinate the spare ribs for at least 1 hour.

When ready for cooking, place a sheet of aluminium foil over a rack and spread the spare ribs over top. Pour over some of the marinade and bake in a moderate oven for approximately 1 hour. Baste occasionally with the remaining marinade.

Note: If the spare ribs are cut into 10 cm lengths, they can be cooked over the barbecue.

CHINESE SALAMI

Larp Cheong

1 pair Chinese salami (beef or chicken liver)
Chinese parsley

Wipe sausages with a warm moist towel, remove string and place on a saucer and steam for 20 minutes.

(continued)

Alternatively, cut into diagonal slivers and place on top of rice during the last ten minutes of steaming.
Garnish with parsley.
Serve as an appetiser or with plain steamed rice.

Note: Chicken liver salami need only be steamed for 15 minutes.

WOOLLY LAMB
Fun See Yong Yuk

500 g cooked lamb
100 g frozen green beans
2 onions
2 tomatoes
1 stalk young celery
1 tablespoon vegetable oil
Salt and pepper
100 g cellophane noodles (fun see)

Sauce:
1 tablespoon soy sauce
½ cup stock (use stock cube)
1 tablespoon cornflour

Use left over lamb from your weekend joint. Cut into approximately 5 cm lengths. Cut the vegetables to a similar size.
Sprinkle ½ teaspoon sugar over cut-up tomatoes.
Heat wock and add vegetable oil when hot. Stir-fry all vegetables and add lamb to heat through. Season with salt and pepper.
Mix soy sauce, stock, blended cornflour in a small bowl and cook into lamb mixture until thickened.
Loosen noodles and cut into lengths to fit into a wock comfortably. Heat oil until blue smoke rises and test a small piece of the noodle first. If the temperature is correct, the noodle will immediately puff up into a snowy white mass. Do not allow to brown.
Ladle lamb mixture on to warm platter and surround with the fried cellophane noodles.

THE NOODLE STORY

Noodles are as common to the northern provinces of China as bread is to the Western world. This is because wheat and its products are plentiful and are used in every conceivable way to produce food. Naturally, noodles and bread are the staple food of the northern peoples.

It is written in history books that in the thirteenth century while Marco Polo was on an expedition to old Cathay he was intrigued by a food that the Chinese always seemed to be consuming. This was the noodle. Noodles and noodle products are still world famous. When Marco Polo returned to Europe and introduced noodles to European countries, they became known as spaghetti, finer noodles as vermecilli, wun tons as ravioli, egg rolls and springs rolls as cannelloni and rice flour products as macaroni.

Home-made noodles (if you have the time) or noodles made by hand by a chef, to me, are the best. When I lived in Shanghai there were places that were strictly allotted to the serving of noodles alone. The chef would come to the table with the dough already to show to his prospective customers. He would then manipulate the dough by swinging it away from each hand until it stretched one to two metres long. This process of noodle swinging required great skill and practice, because doubling the dough over each 'swing' depended on how fine the noodles were to be. Then the dough would be taken into the kitchen and prepared according to whichever process was ordered, either fried, braised or made into soup.

Today, it is the machine age, and naturally, the noodles are more uniform in size. Advancement in marketing has produced a one-person portion dehydrated package together with soup bouillon, which can be brought to the table in five minutes.

The different types and textures of noodles are peculiar to the provinces where they are produced. Noodles from Amoy, or Fukien noodles, are very very fine and come in bundles that can be cooked in a few minutes. As they are so delicate they are recommended for children or older people who cannot readily digest their food, as they are very soft and light when cooked.

In northern China, wheat products are eaten every day either in the form of steamed bread, celestial pancakes or noodles. Dehydrated noodles are fast becoming a familiar sight in the large supermarkets and, owing to the ease with which they can be prepared, are becoming more popular. The most common of the fine noodles are made and twirled into large rings 36 centimetres in diameter and stored packed on top of each other. I find it a marvellous sight to see stacks and stacks of noodles ready to be made into different recipes, together with all the other types.

A little heavier in texture are the noodles made from rice flour. These come in sheets. They can be made into a 'spring roll', steamed and eaten with a dip sauce of soy and sesame seeds. It is a very light snack. They also can be bought fresh and dehydrated in packages where they are wrapped into small bundles about 5 centimetres long and twined together. These must be soaked in cold water for at least one hour before they can be cooked and are called *sar hor fun*.

One of my favourite foods is the transparent noodle, which is made from the mung-bean. It is very fine, with the appearance of bales of thread-like cotton. Being transparent, it is also known as the 'cellophane' noodle. It is used in soups, where it is soaked for ten minutes, becomes very limp and is then added to the soup. It can be braised for use in soups as well. It helps to 'bulk up' a birds' nest soup, as the birds' nest is so expensive and the cellophane noodle is comparatively cheap. When it is deep-fried for a couple of minutes, it becomes very crisp and has a lovely texture when combined with other soft foods. Used as a garnish and sprinkled over food it gives a wonderful crunchy texture to the dish. Cellophane noodles can be kept in an airtight container after deep-frying and stored for one to two weeks.

In restaurants the name of the noodle dish is given according to the type of preparation of the noodles. The more common noodles are made with the addition of eggs and the newest ones on the market have puree of crab or prawn or chicken flavour incorporated in them.

As a general rule 500 g of fresh noodles will serve four people, of course depending on whether they will have side dishes, such as duck or fowl. I find that 500 g of fresh noodles deep-fried produce an enormous mass, but they can be kept quite successfully in an airtight container to be used at a later date. If using noodles and wun ton in a soup, then cut the amount of noodles down to half quantity.

CELLOPHANE NOODLES

100 g cellophane noodles (jun see)
½ cup oil

Separate and cut cellophane noodles into lengths.

Heat oil in wock or frying pan and when blue flame rises, you have the correct temperature to toast noodles.

Gently lower the noodles into the hot oil. They will immediately expand their volume, if the oil is at the correct temperature.

Remove immediately, do not allow them to brown, and drain on absorbent paper. These noodles can be kept in an airtight container.

Note: Test temperature by putting in a small thread of noodle first.

HOME-MADE EGG NOODLES
Lo Mein

500 g high gluten content flour (bread flour)
½ teaspoon salt
3–4 eggs
1 tablespoon water (approximately)
Cornflour for dusting

Sift flour and salt together on pastry board. Make a well and break in the unbeaten eggs. Add water. Make into a dough by mixing the flour into the eggs with your hand. Use more water little by little if too dry, although this dough is a dry one. Knead gently. Allow to stand for 10 minutes.
Sprinkle the board with cornflour and roll out into a very thin paste. Cut into desired widths and lengths. Keep covered when not in use.
To deep-fry noodles, heat oil in a deep pan. Use enough oil to cover the noodles to be cooked. Shake off excess cornflour and gently lower the noodles into oil and deep-fry until golden brown. Drain on absorbent paper. Keep in an air tight container until ready for serving.

CHOW MEIN

500 g fine egg noodles (fresh)
1 teaspoon soy sauce
2–3 teaspoons sesame oil
¼ cup vegetable oil
Filling:
Shrimps
Pork/meats
Chicken/liver/gizzards
Ham
Mushrooms
Chinese cabbage (bark choy)
Water chestnuts
Bamboo shoots
Shredded shallots
Sauce:
1 cup chicken stock
Blended cornflour
Soy sauce
Chili sauce or tabasco
1 tablespoon oyster sauce
Salt and pepper

Boil water in a deep saucepan and gradually put in noodles, keeping the water on the boil. Cook for approximately 3 minutes. Remove and run cold water through them. Drain thoroughly.
Place noodles in a large bowl. Work in the soy sauce and sesame oil. Divide into four parts by placing on a small plate.
Heat vegetable oil in wock and put in one part of noodles. Use a ladle and flatten top to make a large pancake. Brown one side then turn over and brown the other side. Remove to warm platter—this will make one serving.
For the filling combine a selection of the listed meats and vegetables and saute. Add sauce ingredients and heat together. Ladle over the chow mein. Serve hot.

Note: The Chinese prefer their fried noodles crisp on the outside and soft inside.

SUMMER NOODLES

250 g fine noodles
1 tablespoon sesame oil
¼ cooked chicken
Fresh crab meat (substitute 1
  small can crab)
3 slices cooked ham
3 eggs
Shallots
1 tablespoon salad oil
Salt and pepper
2 tablespoons soy sauce

Cook noodles in boiling water until just tender. Remove and drain. Stir in the sesame oil.
Slice chicken into shreds. Flake crab meat. Slice ham.
Beat eggs together and make 3 small omelettes. When cool, cut into shreds.
Strip shallots into 5 cm lengths.
Heat oil in wock and stir noodles around for 3–4 minutes, then add all the meats and omelette shreds and turn gently to mix evenly.
Season with salt, pepper and soy sauce.
Place on large flat platter and sprinkle with strips of shallots. Place in refrigerator to cool for 1 hour before serving.

Note: Serve with a variety of dip sauces as desired.

PORK AND CHICKEN BRAISED NOODLES

500 g noodles
1 cup bean sprouts
1 egg
Cooked chicken (1 breast)
Cooked pork (half a fillet of
  barbecued pork)
1 piece bamboo shoot
Oil for frying
½ cup chicken stock
1 teaspoon soy sauce
Salt and pepper
½ teaspoon sugar
1 tablespoon cornflour
1 teaspoon sesame oil
Chopped shallots

Bring water to boil in a large saucepan and then put in noodles gradually. Allow approximately 6–10 minutes depending on width of noodles. Noodles to be cooked to perfection should be 'bitey', soft outside and elastic inside. The term used is 'al dente'.
Drain in a colander and run cold water through them.
Cut off ends of bean sprouts, wash and drain. Make small omelette with beaten egg and cut into strips. Cut chicken and pork into strips. Cut bamboo shoot into strips.
Heat oil in wock and fry all the ingredients together. Put in chicken stock, soy sauce, salt, pepper and sugar. Add blended cornflour. Remove to a bowl.
Clean wock and add a little extra oil and fry the noodles until heated. Pour in the sesame oil.
Return chicken and pork mixture, turn heat down low, and cover with a lid. Cook for 3–4 minutes. Serve in a large serving dish sprinkled with chopped shallots.

NOODLES WITH HOT SAUCE

300 g egg noodles
250 g minced beef
6 lengths of shallot (white ends)
2 tablespoons vegetable oil
½ teaspoon salt and pepper
1 tablespoon soy sauce
3 tablespoons brown bean paste (min see jeung)
1 tablespoon chili powder (or sauce)
½ cup beef stock (or more)
1 tablespoon sesame oil

Separate egg noodles (if fresh) and plunge into a large pot of boiling water for approximately 10 minutes. (Time required depends on thickness of noodles.) Drain in a colander and run cold water through the noodles.

Chop the minced beef finely (sometimes mince is slightly coarse) together with the shallots.

Heat oil in wock. Put in minced beef, season with salt, pepper and soy sauce and stir-fry until nicely browned. Stir in the brown bean paste and chili powder and continue cooking for 5 minutes.

Pour in stock and stir occasionally. Do not allow to dry out. Reduce heat, cover with a lid and simmer for 20 minutes.

Mix sesame oil through noodles and place in a heated frying pan and heat for 2–3 minutes.

To serve, heat the serving bowl, put in a sprinkling of soy sauce and seasoned vegetable oil, then put in the noodles. Ladle the hot sauce over the top. Garnish with shreds of shallots.

Seasoned Vegetable Oil: Heat ½ cup vegetable oil in the clean wock with a crushed garlic clove and one piece of crushed green ginger. Heat until the garlic is browned, then remove garlic and ginger.

FLAT RICE NOODLES WITH MEAT SAUCE

250 g rice noodles
150 g meat mince
1 onion
1 capsicum
2 tablespoons oil
Salt and pepper
1 tablespoon soy sauce
1 cup stock
1 tablespoon tomato puree
2 tablespoons brown bean paste (min see jeung)
Shallots

Put saucepan of water on to boil and then put in the rice noodles for approximately 8–10 minutes. These rice noodles are cooked soft. Drain.

Mince meat finely. Mix in with chopped onion and capsicum.

Heat oil in wock and fry meat with chopped onion and capsicum. Season with salt and pepper. Add soy sauce.

Pour in stock and tomato puree. Allow to cook for 10 minutes and then put in brown bean paste.

(continued)

Cover with a lid and simmer for 1 hour. Do not allow to become too dry. Correct seasoning.

Serve sauce over the rice noodles. It will have a thick rich pouring consistency. Garnish with shallots.

SOUP NOODLES

250 g egg noodles (fresh or dried)
6 dried mushrooms (or use canned champignons)
Rich chicken stock, seasoned
1 pork chop
1 teaspoon sauce
Salt and pepper
2 teaspoons vegetable oil
1 teaspoon sesame oil (for noodles)
Shallots
Dip sauces

Bring water to boil in a large saucepan and then put in noodles gradually. Allow approximately 10 minutes for thicker type noodles and less time for the finer type. (Fresh noodles will take a shorter time.) Drain in a colander and run cold water through them.

Soak mushrooms in warm water for 20 minutes, then squeeze dry and cut into strips. Put chicken stock on the boil and keep simmering.

Cut off meat from pork chop and cut into strips. Put the bone into the stock. Mix soy sauce, salt, pepper and vegetable oil into strips of pork.

Heat oil in wock and fry pork for 3 minutes, then add the mushrooms. Turn down heat to low, and cover to cook another 2 minutes. Remove to bowl.

Mix sesame oil through the noodles. Clean wock and put in a little extra oil and swirl the noodles around for a couple of minutes.

Have individual bowls ready that have been previously warmed. Put a few drops of vegetable oil and soy sauce at bottom of bowl. Place the noodles in the bowl, a tablespoon or more of the pork and mushrooms. Ladle over the hot steaming soup.

Garnish with strips of shallots. Serve with extra dip sauces.

FRIED FRESH NOODLES

250 g fresh noodles
Oil for deep-frying

Separate fresh noodles.
Heat oil in a deep saucepan and when hot, gradually deep-fry the noodles until golden brown.
Drain well.
Store in an airtight container to be used when required.
To serve, spread noodles on serving dish and spoon desired filling on top.

RICE

By now surely everyone must know that rice is the national dish of China. It is to the Chinese what hot pies are to the Australians and hamburgers to the Americans—a dish no one seems to tire of no matter how often it is served.

The Chinese teach their children not to waste rice. Every grain is to be eaten from the rice bowl. The Chinese hold the bowl in one hand, with the thumb resting on the rim while the base is held firmly with the other fingers. The chopsticks are held in the other hand, and the rice is conveyed to the mouth by bringing the bowl up to the mouth and using the chopsticks as a 'pusher'. Rice is the staff of life and in olden times even wages were calculated in terms of how much rice was earned each month.

Rice is bland in flavour and consequently is an excellent base for the richer flavour Chinese dishes, which are known as *soong*. It is used in the same way as bread with a meal of meat and gravy.

No wonder rice is so highly respected as a food. It is high in carbohydrate content, and unpolished rice has greater nutritive value than any other cereal grain. It also has a digestive capacity of 98 per cent, which makes it one of the more easily digested foods and thus an important source of quick energy. This is probably the reason why Europeans say that they still feel hungry not long after a Chinese meal.

There are thousands of varieties of rice and every housewife has her own favourite way of cooking it. I can only generalize on the method, but a golden rule for success is to wash the rice until the water runs clear and remove any foreign particles or brownish specks. Put the rice in a heavy saucepan with cold water to cover at least 3 cm above the rice level in the pot. Bring to a rapid boil, then reduce heat, cover with a lid and steam for 15 minutes.

Glutinous rice, or 'sticky' rice, has to be soaked for one hour or more before it is cooked. This is one of my favourite foods, especially when it is made into savoury dumplings. The rice is mixed with salty pork, soy beans, smoked pork, eggs or salami, wrapped in lotus leaves and steamed for hours. When unwrapped, the 'sticky' rice is difficult to cut with a knife because the grains of rice stick to the blade. To overcome the problem, use a length of clean string, held taut between both hands and slice through the dumpling. When cold, these slices are fried in a beaten egg mixture and really make good eating, especially in the colder months.

STEAMED RICE

Wash 500 g rice in cold water until the water runs clear. Remove any brown or discoloured grains. Place washed rice in a heavy saucepan with enough cold water to cover the rice level, approximately 3 cm.

Bring to a rolling boil and, as water starts to evaporate and rice appears on top, turn down to the very lowest heat, cover with a lid and steam for 15 minutes.

It is not necessary to stir the rice at all during the cooking period.

Note. An automatic electric rice steamer can be used. I find this method quite satisfactory. Use the same amount of water as prescribed above. It is advisable to stir gently when the water is on the boil.

Left-over Rice: Place in a bowl or colander and steam for 15 minutes or place in a bowl over another dish that is being steamed. The Chinese steam a whole meal in this fashion.

HAM FRIED RICE

500 g long grain rice
2 tablespoons vegetable oil
3 eggs
1 teaspoon salt
150 g cooked ham
1 small can shrimps
1 tablespoon soy sauce
Shallots
Lettuce

Have a large saucepan of water boiling rapidly. Add rice gradually so water does not go off the boil. Boil rapidly uncovered for 12 minutes. Drain well. Spread out on flat tray to dry, then refrigerate.

Heat oil in wock and pour in the beaten eggs. When half set mix in the rice and salt. Lift the rice with the ladle, continuously mixing the grains of rice with the egg.

Add the finely chopped ham and drained shrimps. Continue to fry for 5 minutes.

Sprinkle with soy sauce and mix in the chopped shallots. Correct seasoning.

Have platter with finely shredded lettuce on outside edge. Pile rice on to centre of platter.

Garnish with parsley and a few shrimps.

STEAMED WHITE RICE
(Using electric range)

2 cups rice
Water to cover

Wash rice thoroughly in a deep saucepan and remove any specks of discoloured grain. Pour off as much water as possible. Level the rice in the saucepan and cover with enough cold water to cover by 3 cm.

Switch electric range on to the highest and stir occasionally. When the water starts to evaporate, immediately reduce the heat to the lowest, cover with a lid and allow to steam for 15 minutes.

BUTTER RICE AND SOY SAUCE

1 basin hot steaming rice
2 teaspoons butter
1 teaspoon soy sauce

Mix butter and soy sauce into the hot steaming rice.

Note: This is the equivalent to a plain bread and butter sandwich. Try it, it is delicious. The rice must be piping hot.

FRIED TUNA RICE

4 cups cooked rice, cold
1 small can tuna
3–4 eggs
2 onions
1–2 tablespoons vegetable oil
2 tablespoons cooked green peas (or chopped capsicum)
2 tablespoons soy sauce
Salt and pepper
chopped shallots

Remove any bones and dark skin from the tuna. Using chopsticks or fork, lightly separate tuna meat. Beat eggs together in a bowl.

Peel onions and cut into half lengthwise, then cut very finely into slices, cut side facing downwards. Put oil in wok and swirl around until hot. Fry onion till transparent. Push to one side of wok. Put in rice and turn frequently. Add salt. Continue frying for 5 minutes. Mix in onion.

Make a well in centre of rice, put in little more oil, and pour in the eggs. Stir until almost scrambled, and mix in together with rice and continue frying for a few more minutes.

Add tuna, green peas and soy sauce. Continue frying and mixing in all the ingredients. Correct seasoning.

Serve hot sprinkled with chopped shallots.

SALMON OMELETTE FRIED RICE

3 cups cooked rice (cold)
3 eggs
1 medium size can of salmon
2 onions
¼ cup salad oil
Salt and pepper
1 tablespoon soy sauce

Beat eggs together in a bowl. Discard dark skin and bones from salmon. Reserve liquor. Break up salmon and put half into the beaten eggs, plus 1 tablespoon liquor.

Peel onion and cut into half lengthwise. Place cut surface down on the board and cut into thin slices. Heat oil in wock and when hot, put in 2 tablespoons of the egg and salmon mixture. When the mixture starts to set, put in a few slices of onion and flip over one half of the omelette to make a half-moon shape. Remove and keep warm. Continue to make omelettes until egg mixture is used up.

Add a little more oil if necessary and fry the balance of onions until transparent. Add rice and salt. Turn over rapidly and fry for 5 minutes. Add the balance of flaked salmon and continue to fry for a few more minutes until the salmon is heated through. Sprinkle on soy sauce, correct seasoning. Serve rice on a shallow platter and place the salmon omelettes on top.

Note: For special occasions I sprinkle sweet and sour shreds on top of this rice which makes it a gala dish. Sweet and sour shreds are purchased in jars or cans.

FRIED EGG RICE

3 cups cooked rice
2 tablespoons vegetable oil
Salt and pepper
4 eggs
2 tablespoons soy sauce
Chopped shallots

Separate the grains of the cooked rice with wet chopsticks or a fork.

Heat oil in wock and swirl the oil around. Put in rice, salt and pepper. Fry for 5 minutes.

Beat the other tablespoon of oil lightly with the eggs and pour the mixture on to the rice, turning frequently. Fry for another 10 minutes. This will enable the egg to coat each grain of rice.

Pour on soy sauce and mix in the chopped shallots. Fry for another 5 minutes. Adjust seasoning and serve hot.

Cantonese Fried Rice (p. 91).

SIMPLE FRIED RICE

3 cups cooked rice, cold
3 slices bacon
1 tablespoon vegetable oil
3 eggs
Salt
Chopped shallots
1 tablespoon soy sauce

Separate the grains of rice with a dampened fork. Remove rind from bacon and cut the bacon into shreds. Heat wock and cook bacon until tender—do not crisp. Remove to platter and pour off excess oil to use on another occasion.
Beat eggs together in a bowl.
Heat vegetable oil in wock, pour in the eggs and stir. Before allowing the eggs to set, put in the rice and keep stirring all the time. Add salt.
Return bacon and keep frying for another 5 minutes. Add shallots and sprinkle on the soy sauce, turning frequently.
Serve hot with other main dishes.

RICE SOUP

Pork joint bones and/or chicken or turkey carcass
1 onion
⅓ cup uncooked rice
12–15 pork and veal rissoles (see recipe on page 15)
Few lettuce leaves
Shallots

Place bones and/or carcass in a large saucepan with enough water to cover. Add cut-up onion and washed rice and bring to the boil. Simmer for 30 minutes. Allow to stand overnight. Next day, remove fat from top and bones.
Bring to the boil again and gently put in tiny rissoles to cook. They will rise to the top when they are ready. Dip lettuce into the hot soup until it becomes transparent. Put in the chopped shallots and add salt to taste.
To serve, sprinkle a few drops of soy sauce and sesame oil on the bottom of soup bowl. Add 3–4 rissoles and lettuce. Spoon over the hot soup.

BREAKFAST EGGS

Eggs
1 teaspoon vegetable oil per egg
Chopped shallots
½ teaspoon soy sauce
Dash sesame oil
Hot steamed rice

Heat wock and swirl the oil around. When hot, break in each egg separately.
When the egg starts to set, sprinkle the yolk with chopped shallots and baste with the hot oil.
Have warm plate with hot steamed rice ready and place eggs on top of rice. Spoon over the soy sauce and sesame oil.

Brandied Roast Pork (p. 67).

STEAMED RICE WITH CHICKEN
Gai Ko Farn

½ spring chicken
1 tablespoon soy sauce
1 teaspoon oyster sauce (hor yo)
½ teaspoon salt
1 tablespoon rose wine (mui gwa lo)
Shredded green ginger
3 cups rice
2½ cups water approximately

Few slices of hard vegetable (celery, bamboo shoot, broccoli, mustard cabbage)

Prepare chicken by cleaning and chop into large pieces, going through the bone. Place in a bowl with the soy sauce, oyster sauce, salt, rose wine and shredded ginger. Allow to marinate for 30 minutes.

Wash rice thoroughly and place it in a large saucepan. Cover with water to approximately 3 cm over rice level. Bring to the boil over high heat, and when water is starting to evaporate, add the chicken to the rice.

Turn to lowest heat, cover with tight fitting lid and steam for 20 minutes. During the last five minutes, add the cut-up vegetable.

Serve piping hot.

Note: This is a classical Cantonese dish.

ALMOND FRIED RICE

4 cups cooked rice, cold
½ cup slivered almonds
1 cup vegetable oil
4 eggs
1 teaspoon salt
3 slices cooked ham
Chopped shallots
1 tablespoon soy sauce
Chinese parsley

Wet fork and work through cold rice so as to separate grains.

Fry slivered almonds in hot oil until golden brown. Drain.

Beat eggs together in a small bowl. Cut ham into long lengths resembling the size of almond slivers. Drain most of the oil from cooking of the almonds and heat up again. Pour in the eggs, stirring all the time.

Immediately put in the rice and salt. Continue to fry the rice by lifting rapidly to enable the egg to coat the grains of rice. Fry for another 5 minutes. Add ham, shallots and soy sauce, continually stirring and mixing. Just before serving, fold in most of the toasted almond slivers.

Serve immediately on warm platter. Garnish with remaining toasted almonds and Chinese parsley.

MIXED SALAMI FRIED RICE

3 cups cooked rice, cold
2 eggs
1 tablespoon vegetable oil
Mixed salami, Devon or
    Windsor sausage
1 onion
½ cup cooked green peas
1 tablespoon soy sauce
Salt and pepper

Make two omelettes with beaten eggs and when cool enough to handle, cut into small dice. Cut the salami and onion into same size.
Put a little oil in the wock and when hot, gently fry the onion. Add rice, and keep on turning the rice over continuously to fry.
Add cooked green peas, and meats and fry another 5 minutes. Sprinkle with soy sauce, add the egg, frying all the time. Correct seasoning.
Serve hot.

FRIED RICE WITH LEFT-OVER LAMB

3 cups cooked rice, cold
Pieces of left-over lamb from
    the weekend joint
Salt and oil
1 large onion
2–3 eggs
Chopped shallots
1 tablespoon soy sauce
1 tablespoon vegetable oil

Separate cold grains of rice with a wet fork.
Heat oil in wock, fry the onion and then sear the cut up pieces of lamb. Remove.
Add a little more oil, and when hot, pour in the beaten eggs to make two omelettes. When cool, cut into shreds.
Heat the wock again, add rice and salt. Fry for 5 minutes by turning up the rice and turning the wock around.
Mix in the lamb and onions. Fry for another 5 minutes.
Correct seasoning, then put in shallots and soy sauce and heat the egg shreds. Keep turning over frequently.
Serve while hot.

SALTED DUCK EGGS

1 egg per person
1 teaspoon hot vegetable oil
½ teaspoon sesame oil

Remove the coating of black clay from the egg and wash clean. Place in a saucepan of cold water and cook for 15–20 minutes. Remove and run under cold tap to cool.
Peel off shell and cut into quarters. Pour over the hot vegetable oil and sesame oil.
Eat with plain boiled rice.

GLUTINOUS RICE DUMPLINGS
Joong

2 kg glutinous rice (nor mei
  fun)
Dried lotus leaves
Length of twine
250 g white or red soy beans
100 g pork fat (preserved in
  salt at least for 24 hours)
6 salted duck's eggs
100 g diced cooked pork

Wash rice and soak for 1 hour (or more) with enough water to cover completely. Pour off excess water and place in a large bowl.

Soak lotus leaves in hot water to make pliable and sterilize the twine. Soak soy beans overnight to soften. Dice the pork fat.

Separate the yolks from the egg whites and put them in a small basin. Mix salt and soy beans into glutinous rice.

Using 3–4 lotus leaves make a cone shape and spoon in 4 tablespoons of the rice mixture, press in a cube of pork, cover with rice mixture, press in egg yolk. Continue alternating pork and rice. Press down tightly with the back of a dessert spoon. Close with another lotus leaf and tie the whole dumpling with twine.

Place dumplings in a large saucepan with warm water to cover and bring to the boil then simmer for 4–5 hours, depending on how many are cooking at the one time. Reheat in the same pot and water the next day and simmer for another hour.

Serve hot, or when cold, dip into beaten eggs and fry until golden brown on both sides.

CHICKEN LIVER RICE

500 g rice
2½ cups water (approximately)
1 pair chicken liver salami (or
  cooked chicken livers)

Wash rice in cold water three or four times until water is clear. Place in a deep saucepan and cover with cold water 3 cm above rice level in the saucepan. Put on the highest heat and bring to the boil. When most of the water has evaporated, place cut up chicken liver salami on top and push into rice.

Reduce heat to lowest, cover with a tight fitting lid and steam for another 15–20 minutes.

Serve in separate bowls with pieces of salami.

Note: Salami is bought at the Chinese food stores and comes in pairs. This is a classical dish of the Cantonese province.

CANTONESE FRIED RICE

450 g cooked rice
2 slices smoked ham
3 eggs
2 tablespoons vegetable oil
1 teaspoon salt
½ cup cooked prawns
2 lengths of shallots
1 tablespoon soy sauce

Fork through cooked rice to remove any small lumps. Slice ham. Beat eggs together.
Heat vegetable oil in wock or frying pan and when hot, pour in beaten eggs. When egg is half set, mix in rice and stir rapidly so egg starts to coat the grains of rice. Add ham, chopped shallots and shelled prawns. (Reserve a few prawns for garnishing.) Sprinkle with soy sauce and continue frying until golden in colour. Adjust seasoning. Serve hot on platter with a garnish of prawns.

FIRECRACKER RICE

Firecracker rice is made using the crusts formed on the bottom of the saucepan when short grain rice is cooked over very high heat so as to 'set' the bottom layer of rice.

After all the steamed rice is used, break the crusts from the bottom of the pan into small pieces and place on a baking tray and dry out in the oven using very low heat.

When completely dry, deep-fry in oil until golden brown.

These pieces are used in soups and other dishes. When the hot soup is poured over the crust of firecracker rice, it will sizzle and explode happily.

Alternatively, to make a refreshing light 'tea', water is poured on top of the crust, seasoned and allowed to simmer for 20 minutes. This is usually served after a meal.

DESSERTS

WONG'S BOMBE

Sponge cake base (oblong shape)
Plain vanilla ice-cream (oblong shape)
500 g fresh lychees or 1 can lychees
Preserved ginger in syrup
Few strawberries
Egg whites
Brandy
Sparklers

Place sponge cake base on heat proof platter. Sprinkle with brandy.

Slice ice-cream block into lengths approximately 5 cm high and when softened enough, place peeled lychees on top interspersed with shredded preserved ginger. Cover with another layer of ice-cream. Place strawberries on top interspersed with shredded preserved ginger. Cover with another layer of ice-cream.

Have egg white whipped to a stiff meringue, and cover the ice-cream with this mixture, making sure that the bottom ends are well covered. Push half an egg shell into top of meringue.

Place in hot oven to brown meringue slightly.

Place 3 sparklers at each end. Pour warmed brandy into egg shell. Present with sparklers lit and then ignite brandy. Serve immediately.

Note: This is a wonderful dessert for a Chinese New Year's party, but it must have immediate attention and correct timing.

LYCHEE SPECIAL

1 can lychees
Honeydew melon
Watermelon
Champagne (substitute syrup from lychees)

Drain lychees. Cut honeydew melon and watermelon into balls with a melon baller.

Combine three fruits into a tall glass and pour in champagne.

Note: This dish is especially good with fresh lychees when they are available.

ALMOND FLOAT WITH COCKTAIL FRUITS

1 small bundle agar-agar (approximately 15 g)
5 cups water
1 tablespoon castor sugar
½ cup evaporated milk
Almond essence
Fruit cocktail
Fresh cream

Spread out the agar-agar in a deep bowl and wash through to remove any particles of dust. Squeeze dry and place in a saucepan with water. Heat through until dissolved, approximately 15 minutes, stirring continuously.

Turn heat down to low and stir in the sugar and evaporated milk. Mix in a few drops of almond essence.

Pour on a flat tray and allow to cool. Cut into shapes and place in a large serving bowl with a few cubes of ice.

Stir in the fruit cocktail and fruit syrup.

Serve in separate bowls with a rosette of fresh cream topping each dish.

Note: Substitute gelatine. The value of using agar-agar is that it sets so quickly and it is not necessary to place it in the refrigerator.

FRESH COCONUT MILK

The water in the coconut is not the coconut milk used in cooking. When the coconut is peeled of its fibres, break it in half and remove the flesh by hand with a sharp knife or an implement that is designed especially for this purpose. Amongst my kitchen equipment, I have a primitive type which was purchased in Malaysia. It is shaped in a half-curve and one end clamps on to a solid surface. At the curved end there is a sharp cutter with grooves on the ends. The half of the coconut is pushed against the sharp ends and the flesh is churned out.

Cover the grated flesh with water, mix together by hand and allow to stand a while. Squeeze out all the white liquor to make the fresh coconut cream. Add water to the remains for a second time to make the coconut milk.

Coconut milk can be used as stock when there is an abundance of fresh coconuts.

COCONUT CREAM FROM DESICCATED COCONUT

Place desiccated coconut in a large bowl and pour in enough warm water to cover. Allow to stand 30 minutes or longer. Using a fine sieve, squeeze all the liquor from the coconut. A fine piece of muslin may be placed over the sieve to prevent any particles of coconut seeping through. The first liquor is called the coconut cream. Using the residue of desiccated coconut pour in another 1 or 2 cups of warm water and allow to stand another 30 minutes. Squeeze out the liquor again, and this becomes the coconut milk.

CHILLED WATERMELON BASKET

1 elongated watermelon
1 honeydew melon
20–30 fresh lychees (sub-stitute 1 medium size can)
12 fresh loquats
Red cherries
Preserved kumquats

Cut melon lengthwise leaving a handle in centre to resemble a basket. Scoop out red pulp, remove seeds and with a melon baller, shape pulp into balls.
With a sharp knife serrate the edge of the 'basket' to make it look more attractive.
Peel skin from honeydew melon and shape the pulp into balls. Arrange all the fruits in the basket mixing the colours. Chill.
Before serving, pour 1 or 2 cups chilled champagne over the fruit.

DRAGON SEED COCKTAIL
(Loong Narn)

1 large can loong narn (dragon seeds)
1 small bottle champagne or sparkling white wine
Strawberries or cherries (in season)
Preserved ginger

Drain loong narn and place in chilled serving bowl. Pour over the champagne and chill for half an hour.
Serve each person with about 10 pieces of loong narn and add strawberries or cherries.
Garnish with sliced slivers of preserved ginger.

Note: Loong narn are small white flesh fruits, crisp and sweet, the brother to the lychee.

CHECKERBOARD

1 small bundle agar-agar (approx 15 g)
5 cups water
2 tablespoons castor sugar
½ cup canned milk
Almond essence
1 can lemon grass jelly
Fruit syrup
Cherries
Strawberries and leaves

Spread out the agar-agar in a deep bowl and wash through to remove any particles of dust. Squeeze dry and place in a saucepan with water. Heat through until dissolved, approximately 15 minutes, stirring continuously.

Turn heat down to low and stir in the sugar and milk. Mix in the few drops of almond essence.

Pour into a flat tray and allow to cool. Cut into squares and place into a large serving bowl with a few cubes of ice.

Cut up lemon grass in same size cubes and mingle together. Pour in any syrup from canned fruits and/or sweet champagne.

Use a few red cherries or strawberries to decorate, as well as strawberry leaves, to make an impressive looking dessert.

Note: Lemon grass jelly is a translucent, dark brown jelly. When you open the can just cut the jelly in half and turn out. Cut into squares.

SAVOURY TARO TART

500 g taro (substitute sweet potato or potatoes)
2 cups glutinous flour (nor mei fun) (substitute rice flour and cornflour ratio 3:1)
200 g cooked pork
Salt
½ cup dried shrimps (har mei)
1 piece salted vegetable (choong choy)
Chopped shallots

Peel and cut taro root into small dice. Boil in water until just tender. Drain.

Mix flour and mashed taro root together, using any liquor left from cooking the taro. Stir in the diced pork, enveloping it in the dough. Add salt to taste.

Pour dough into an oiled shallow cake tin, garnish with washed dried shrimps and sprinkle with chopped salted vegetable and shallots. Steam for 1 hour, or until mixture cooks and sets. When cool, cut into squares.

Substitute recipe: Use sweet potatoes or potatoes. Mix three parts rice flour and one part cornflour. Garnish on top with chopped bacon, ham, shallots, onion or celery.

CUMQUAT DESSERT

1 can cumquats
1 length agar–agar
2 cups water
2 tablespoons sugar
2 tablespoons brandy

Dissolve agar–agar in water, bring to the boil and strain through muslin.

Pour syrup from cumquats and combine with water and sugar in small saucepan. Bring to the boil. Stir in agar–agar. Add brandy. Allow to cool slightly.

Have a mould ready. Use a tray which makes round ice cubes. Place a cumquat in each section. Spoon the syrup over the cumquat. Work quickly before agar–agar sets.

CHINESE STYLE SPONGE CAKES

3–4 eggs
½ cup castor sugar
½ cup milk
1 cup flour
½ teaspoon baking powder
Pinch salt
2 tablespoons lard or shortening
3 tablespoons salad oil

Beat eggs together, add sugar and continue beating until mixture has the consistency of thick cream, as for a sponge cake. Add milk.

Fold in sifted flour, baking powder and salt.

Melt lard and when cool mix into vegetable oil. Gently stir into mixture.

Spoon mixture into small greased containers and steam for 15–20 minutes.

Remove cakes from the container while hot.

WALNUT TEA

1 kg shelled walnuts
½ cup vegetable oil
1 litre water
1 cup sugar (to taste)
Pinch salt
5–6 tablespoons cornflour

Place walnuts in a small saucepan, cover with water and bring to the boil for 10 minutes. Remove and allow to cool. Remove skin from walnuts and drain dry on absorbent paper.

Heat oil in wock and fry walnuts until golden brown. Be careful not to overcook them. When cool, grind in blender or crush with a rolling pin until very fine.

Bring water to the boil with sugar and salt added. Put in the ground walnuts. Keep stirring all the while and thicken with blended cornflour.

To serve, ladle into small bowls and eat while warm.

Note: This tea is usually served after a banquet of many courses. An alternative is Almond Tea.

GOURMET DISHES

LOBSTER AND CRAB DUMPLINGS

Sui mei

150 g lobster meat
100 g canned crab
2 slices ham fat
Salt and pepper
1 piece bamboo shoot
Chinese transparent pastry
  (see recipe p. 20)

Combine the lobster and crab meat. Chop the ham fat into a coarse mince and mix into lobster. Season.
Cut the bamboo shoot into small dice.
Have pastry rolled into 8 cm rounds.
Place a teaspoon of the lobster mixture and ½ teaspoon bamboo shoot in centre of pastry, making pleats on one half, then sealing the pastry together securely.
Steam for 10 minutes. Serve hot or cold with a soy sauce dip.

CAULIFLOWER ROLLS

Cauliflower
Bacon rashers
Toothpicks
Sauce:
2 cups stock (from stock cube)
2 tablespoons cornflour
1 teaspoon soy sauce
1 tablespoon oyster sauce
100 g crab meat
1 egg yolk

Cut cauliflower into small flowerets. Wash and drain.
Cut bacon into strips long enough to wind around flowerets. Secure with a toothpick. Place in a shallow heatproof tray.
Pour boiling water over flowerets and poach over slow heat for 10 minutes, or until cauliflower is tender. Gently pour away excess water. Place under griller to crisp bacon tops.
To make the sauce, place stock on medium heat and bring to the boil. Blend in cornflour and soy sauce. Stir into stock until thickened, then put in oyster sauce and crab meat. Beat egg yolk lightly and stir in just before serving.
Cover cauliflower with the crab and oyster sauce. Serve hot with the main dish.

MANDARIN DUCK

1 1½–2 kg fat duck
Oil for deep-frying
1 piece mandarin skin (dried)
Water to cover
½ cup soy sauce
½ cup sherry
1 teaspoon salt
1 small can mandarin segments in syrup
2 tablespoons cornflour
Shallot flowers (see page p. 38)

Clean duck and tie feet together with string, leaving enough over to be able to hold the duck securely. Dip duck in a large pan of boiling water 4–5 times. This will plump the duck. Drain and pat dry.

Deep-fry duck by using two large woks or deep saucepans. With enough oil for deep-frying in one wock, ladle the hot oil over duck in the other. Reverse the procedure until duck is golden brown. At this stage the duck does not have to be thoroughly cooked.

Keep the duck in one saucepan pouring off any excess oil. Add the mandarin skin, water, soy sauce, sherry and salt. Simmer for approximately 40 minutes or until duck is tender. Carefully remove to a deep casserole and keep warm.

Take out the mandarin skin and shred finely. Pour in the mandarin syrup and cook for 1 minute.

Stir in blended cornflour and cook until thickened. Return shredded mandarin skin.

To serve, place mandarin segments around duck and spoon over the sauce. Garnish with shallot flowers.

To dry mandarin skin: Cut from top to bottom, without cutting right through, in four sections the skin from a mandarin or a tangerine. Remove fruit and eat. Thread a string through bottom of mandarin skin and hang in the sun for two weeks. When completely dehydrated, put into a tight top jar. It will keep indefinitely.

ROAST PORK CANTONESE STYLE

2–3 kg loin of pork
1 teaspoon salt
2 tablespoons Chinese salted vegetable (choong choy)

Rub the skin of pork well with salt. Cut the underside in 3–4 places and pat in the salted vegetable. Curve slightly.

Put pork on a wire rack which is covered with aluminium foil and stand on a baking dish. Place in a hot oven for the first 15 minutes of cooking to enable the skin to become crisp. Then reduce heat to moderate and continue cooking the pork, approximately 1½ hours.

(continued)

To serve, cut off the crackling and break into pieces, then slice pork when cool enough to handle.

Note: The Chinese vegetable gives an unusual flavour to the pork and I cannot recommend any substitute.

FRESH CRAB WITH GINGER SAUCE

1 large mud crab
1 large piece fresh green ginger
1 clove garlic
½ beef stock cube in 1 tablespoon water
3–4 tablespoons strips of shallots

Wash and scrub crab thoroughly. Remove whole shell and discard fibres. Chop crab into 6 sections leaving the legs attached. Place in a casserole ready for steaming.
Peel and shred the green ginger finely. Sprinkle on top of cut-up crab. Add the crushed garlic and stock cube. Steam for 20 minutes. During the last minute of cooking, sprinkle strips of shallots on top.
Serve with Worcestershire sauce and have a finger bowl ready.

CURRIED PRAWNS MALAYSIAN

1 kg king size fresh prawns
2 onions, minced
4 tablespoons vegetable oil
1 cup coconut milk
Green salad

Curry Ingredients:
½ teaspoon turmeric
½ teaspoon mustard
½ cup peanut butter
4–5 red hot chilis
1 tablespoon curry powder
½ teaspoon five spice
1 teaspoon anchovy paste (blanchan)
Lemon grass
1 tablespoon sesame oil
1 tablespoon sesame paste

Remove intestinal track from back of prawns and wash heads thoroughly. Cut in three sections.
Grind the curry ingredients together and mix into prawns.
Heat oil in wock and saute onions until transparent, add prawns and when they turn pink, pour in the coconut milk. Simmer for 5 minutes, stirring occasionally.
Serve with a green salad of lettuce, cucumbers and celery.

Note: This curry is a dry type, not one with a lot of sauce. The reason I give the recipe for making your own curry is so that you may capture the authentic Malaysian taste. For convenience, use your favourite brand of curry powder or paste.

MINCED PIGEON

500 g pigeon meat
100 g minced pork
2–3 chicken livers
Salt and pepper
1 egg yolk
2 tablespoons rose wine or sherry
1 tablespoon cornflour
10 water chestnuts
6 mushrooms
2 tablespoons vegetable oil
200 g transparent noodles

Sauce:
½ cup seasoned stock
2 teaspoons soy sauce
½ teaspoon salt
1 teaspoon sesame oil
2 tablespoons cornflour
Lettuce

Mince the pigeon, pork and chicken livers into a coarse mince. Place in a bowl and mix in salt, egg yolk, sherry and cornflour.

Chop up water chestnuts and prepared mushrooms into tiny dice and add to the pigeon mixture. Season with salt and pepper.

Heat oil in wock or frying pan and saute pigeon mince for approximately 5 minutes, or until cooked. Remove and keep warm in a deep casserole.

Put the sauce ingredients into wock and cook until thickened, then return pigeon mince to heat through.

Use a clean wock or deep saucepan and deep fry the noodles until they puff, but ensure that they do not brown. This only takes a few seconds if the oil is hot enough.

Endeavour to have washed lettuce leaves in uniform curved pieces.

Serve the pigeon on a warm platter surrounded with the puffed fried noodles. Spoon the pigeon mixture into the lettuce cup and eat with the fingers.

STUFFED EGGPLANTS

Eggplants
Round, ball squash
1 onion
2 slices cooked ham
1 boiled potato
1 clove garlic
Salt
Grated cheese
1 egg
Breadcrumbs

Boil the eggplants and/or squash in salted water with the cut-up onion. When tender, but still whole, drain and cut in halves. Spoon out the soft inside and save.

Mince ham with the onion saved from the cooking of the eggplant and boiled potato. Add crushed garlic, if desired. Mix together with the vegetable that has been spooned out and season with salt and a little grated cheese. Bind together with beaten egg.

Spoon this filling into the eggplant and/or squash shells. Top with cheese and breadcrumbs and put under a griller or hot oven to cook until brown on top.

Serve hot or cold.

The next five recipes are included in this cookbook because, while I was chasing recipes on my last gourmet tour, the Palace of Monaco gave me these recipes to use as I desired, and so I have placed them in this section.

PISSALADIERE

500 g flour
15–20 g of yeast
2 tablespoons salad or olive oil
½ cup milk (approximately)
Pinch salt

Sauce Ingredients:
4–5 onions, cut into rings
3 tablespoons concentrated tomato paste mixed with water
Few anchovies
Garlic
Olives

Sift flour in a large bowl. Dissolve yeast in a little water and add to flour. Make a light dough using the olive oil and little milk. Add salt. Allow to rest until the dough has risen three-quarters of its volume.

To make the sauce, fry the onion rings in oil until golden brown and mix in the concentrated tomato. (You can use 4–5 fresh tomatoes and cook with the onion rings.)

Roll out dough to thickness of 1 cm and put on a large oiled pizza tray. Pour cooled sauce over the dough, decorate with anchovies, minced garlic and olives.

Place in moderate oven and cook for approximately 20–30 minutes.

Serve cold.

ZUCCHINI PIE

3–4 green zucchini
2 onions
2 tablespoons salad or vegetable oil
Salt and pepper
200 g cooked white rice
3 eggs
Grated Parmesan cheese

Short pastry:
400 g flour
200 g salad or olive oil
Some water
Salt

Make short pastry with flour, olive oil, water and salt. Roll out to a thin layer and cover an oiled oven slide tray.

Peel the green zucchini and cut into small dice. Mince the onions.

Heat oil in a fry pan and brown the vegetables together. Add salt and pepper and allow to simmer for 5–10 minutes or until the zucchini is nearly cooked. Mix in cooked rice and cook a further 5 minutes.

Cover pastry with the mixture of vegetables and rice. Pour over beaten eggs and sprinkle with cheese. Top this with another thin layer of pastry and seal the edges well.

Bake in moderate oven for approximately 1 hour. Serve cold.

STUFFED SARDINES

1½ kg big and fresh sardines
Parsley
Lemon

Stuffing:
200 g Swiss chard, washed, dried and finely cut
1 clove garlic
2 shallot bulbs or 1 small onion
200 g grated Parmesan cheese
3 eggs
Nutmeg
Fresh breadcrumbs (optional)

Mix all the stuffing ingredients together and add a little fresh breadcrumbs soaked in milk (optional). Wash and clean sardines and pack filling in each one.
Roll each sardine in sifted flour and pan-fry till golden brown.
Serve with a garnish of parsley and lemon wedges.

Note: Swiss chard is a variety of beet which has large leaves and succulent stalks. I suggest a substitute of any green cabbage or spinach.

MONEGASQUE TILLANS

Firm tomatoes
Large onions
Squash, round type
Egg plants
Stuffing:
200 g veal and pork mince
2 tablespoons salad or olive oil
1 clove garlic
Parsley
Basil
Grated Parmesan cheese
Breadcrumbs
2 eggs

Cut the tomatoes in half and put them in the oven for 15 minutes. Scoop out pulp and save.
Boil the onions, squash and eggplants in salted water until tender, but still whole. Scoop out pulp and save.
Fry minced meat in a little salad or olive oil, add chopped clove of garlic, chopped parsley, a sprinkle of basil, grated Parmesan cheese and breadcrumbs. Season to taste. Mix in the vegetable pulps and bind mixture with beaten eggs.
Stuff the vegetables with this mixture. Sprinkle with breadcrumbs and cheese and put under griller or oven to brown on top.
Serve warm.

DRIED SCALLOP SOUP

8–10 dried scallops
2 cups water
1½ litres chicken stock
Salt and pepper
2 tablespoons frozen green peas
2 eggs
Chinese parsley

Wipe scallops with a warm cloth and put them in a small saucepan with water to cover and bring to the boil. Simmer 20 minutes. Pull the strands of scallops apart.
Bring the chicken stock to the boil in a large saucepan, season with salt and pepper. Pour in the scallops and any liquor remaining. Add the frozen

(continued)

Lychee Special (p. 92).

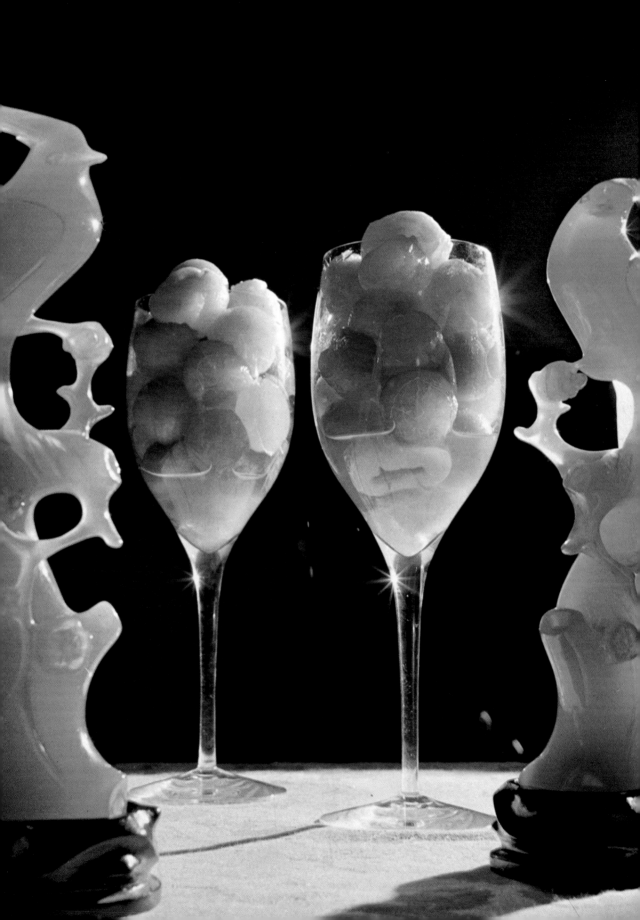

peas.

Beat eggs lightly in a small bowl. Pour the beaten egg slowly through the prongs of a fork, moving the fork so that the egg covers the surface of the soup. Stir gently to form flower pattern.

Serve the hot soup in a soup tureen garnished with leaves of Chinese parsley.

CANTONESE SPICED PORK

2 kg fresh belly pork
Soup vegetables
1½ teaspoons salt
3 tablespoons soy sauce
Oil for deep-frying
2 cloves garlic
3 tablespoons red bean curd
1 teaspoon five spice powder
2 tablespoons soy sauce
4 tablespoons brandy
2 tablespoons salted vegetable (choong choy)
Shallots
Chinese parsley

Place the whole piece of pork in a large saucepan with enough water to cover, add the cut-up vegetables and boil for 5–20 minutes.

Have ready a second saucepan of cold water. Using a large fork, secure the pork firmly and plunge the pork into the cold water. Repeat the process of plunging into the boiling water and then into the cold water 3 or 4 times. Remove and drain. Prick the skin with a fork which will release excess liquid. (Retain soup as stock base.)

Rub salt and soy sauce over the cool pork. Allow to stand 15 minutes. Deep-fry the pork in a deep saucepan, skin side down first, until crisp. Be careful of the oil splattering. Then immediately cover with a lid and cook over slow heat for 10 minutes.

Remove pork and, when cool enough to handle, cut into thin 5 cm slices. Place in a casserole ready for steaming with skin side downwards.

Gently crush garlic in a bowl, mix in the red bean curd, five spice powder, soy sauce, salt and brandy. Blend to a paste and spoon over the sliced pork. Spoon the salted vegetable on top and steam for approximately 1–1½ hours or until pork is tender. Serve hot by turning out onto a platter, when the skin will be on top. Garnish with shallot flowers and Chinese parsley.

Top: Fish Cakes (p. 50) and Fish Balls are made from the same mixture. Fish Cakes are gently fried, Fish Balls are added to soups. Bottom: Chicken Pieces with Lemon Sauce (p. 58).

TEAS

The ten thousand feelings in the mind
Are transformed to Spring
Only the tip of the brush can draw
The spirit as well as a figure.

It is interesting to know that *Cha* (tea) and *Ma* (mother) are similar in sound in every language around the world, and these words are used practically every day. So, for the method of making tea every day, here are a few points to keep in mind if you want to produce a decent brew with good body and flavour.

The water should be boiled just to the boiling point. If it is allowed to keep boiling, it loses its oxygen content and this will impair the taste of the tea. Next, the teapot should be preheated and brought close to where the water is boiling. Your choice of teapot can run to the best china, porcelain or silver.

It is imperative that the water be at boiling point so that when it touches the tea leaves and infusion begins, the greater part of the tea leaves will float on top. Then the tea leaves on the bottom will rise to the top and the top leaves will sink to the bottom. Infusion will take three to four minutes, when all the tea leaves will have sunk to the bottom. If the water is not at a rolling boil, most of the tea leaves will float during the infusion. The rest of the tea leaves will remain at the bottom and there will be little movement of tea leaves so that it will be impossible to obtain the full flavour of the tea. When the water is left boiling and then used to make tea, the tea leaves will sink to the bottom at the start of infusion, and the result will be a weak, poor flavoured brew.

Tea drinking is a ritual in Chinese culture. Chinese tea is served all day long in the home and at special tea-houses there are many varieties to choose from fragrant to medicinal teas. The main types of tea grown in China all come from the same tea plant but the leaves are processed differently. The tender leaves are used for 'green' tea, and the other leaves are processed to produce 'black' or 'red' tea. These teas are made more fragrant with the addition of chrysanthemums, rose petals, jasmine, lotus and plum blossoms, lychee and other fragrant flowers. These teas are taken without sugar and milk as the tea itself is quite scented and refreshing. One teaspoon of tea to six cups of water is the usual quantity used but this differs according to individual taste.

Before the arrival of vacuum flasks, every household had a wicker basket which was padded inside and fitted snugly with a china teapot and tiny cups without handles, to hold the hot tea to see the family through the day. My father was a great tea drinker and his first favourite was Foo Mei Cha, which was a black tea and came compressed in large round shapes. His second favourite was Luk On Cha, which was also a black tea and came packed in small oval baskets. Whenever my mother felt a cold coming on she would brew a pot of Kam Wo Cha, which is tea mixed with Chinese herbs, and sip this all day. This tea comes in tiny packets and one of these is used to six cups of water. The taste is slightly bitter.

Chinese tea has a very delicate flavour and is translucent and so it is believed that drinking lots of tea will keep the complexion fine and clear. It is imperative to have a cup of piping hot tea at the end of every meal, so soothing to the system after one has eaten satisfactorily. There is also warming-the-system tea, cooling-the-system tea, stimulating-the-senses tea, scented and flower petal tea, sweet–bitter–almond tea, lemon-grass jelly fruit tea and now the instant medicinal tea bag!

One of the duties of a new bride in China is the ceremony of personally pouring tea for all the guests at her wedding, whom she serves one at a time. In return she is handed a 'lee see', a lucky red packet containing money. What a lovely way to meet all the guests.

WINE LIST

In the beginning drinking wine was restricted solely to the Emperors, warlords and high ranking officials of the Court. This society of Mandarins were among the richest in the land and they could afford to distill rice and grain for making wine as well as using them for food.

Legend has it that the discovery of wine in China took place when a chef in the Imperial household soaked some rice in an earthenware container and forgot about it. A few days later when he discovered it, he tasted the rice which was delicious. Then he decided to taste the liquor which was even better. It tasted so good that he drank more, and he found that the more he drank, the happier he became. When the Emperor heard of this he called all his advisers together for a meeting and for tasting the wine, The meeting had to be abandoned, because after sampling the wine, they were in no condition for serious business, so the Emperor decreed that:

- Wine must be drunk in small cups and not large bowls
- No one was to drink on an empty stomach and that wine was to be taken between courses
- While drinking wine, the mind must be kept busy and this is possibly the reason why the 'fingers' game is so popular at parties.

The 'fingers' game of *Chi* is played by two people or two sides who elect a leader to represent them. The game must be played in sing-song rhythm. Each person thrusts out a hand denoting a number by his fingers. Both players call the total of both hands. The loser does the drinking and so the game goes on well through the night at large gatherings.

In the north of China where the winters are long and cold, the rice wine is served warm. It is surprising to learn that rice wine is so strong, and warming it renders it all the more potent. (To warm the rice wine, transfer it to a porcelain container and place in enough water to reach the level of the rice wine. When the water heats up, allow it to simmer gently for a few minutes.) Saki, the well-known rice wine, is warmed before serving. It is poured from porcelain or silver containers into tiny wine cups without handles.

There is a lot more interest in recent years in Chinese wines by consumers abroad. Perhaps this has been brought about by travel into China proper being more easily allowed and by the publicity derived from the effects of the Moutai cocktail. This cocktail has Moutai Chiew as the base and is mixed with Wu Chia Pi (90 per cent alcohol proof). It is indeed a 'firecracker'. A milder Moutai cocktail is made from Moutai Chiew and a blend of six to twelve different brandies and added spices. It is a marvellous dinner drink and is certainly a great way to start a party.

Chinese wines are distilled twice or three times, thus their names 'Sheung Jing' (twice distilled) and 'Sam Jing' (three times distilled). They are made from rice, glutinous rice, millet, sorghum and other grains.

One of the lesser known wines which is pale amber in colour is made from fermented glutinous rice and is called 'Shantung'. This is used in the cooking of game and game birds. This name is also given to one of the most famous silks in the world that is made in this region.

No self-respecting chef would admit to being without a bottle of Mei Kuei Lu in his kitchen. It has the fragrance of roses which gives the wine a delicate and refreshing bouquet. When used in vegetable dishes instead of water or stock, it transforms an ordinary dish into one in the gourmet class.

It is only on rare occasions that the Chinese serve wine with their daily meals. I remember when my father would entertain a guest or a family at home, they would sip wine during the whole of the meal instead of having the traditional bowl of rice. At the end of the meal they would finish off with a steaming bowl of rice. There would be a choice of Sam Jing Chiew, Sheung Jing Chiew, Mei Kuei Lu Chiew, Ng Gar Pei or other brandies and whiskies.

The fruit liqueurs are not as well-known to the West, but the Chinese have a large variety made from apricots, plums, pears, oranges and cherries (known to be the largest in the world) that are grown in China.

Other wines that are plentiful are the medicinal wines that are made from snakes, birds, tiger bones, elephant tusks, monkey glands and rhinoceros. I have seen the wine maker come to our dining table with a specially bred snake. He expertly gauges just where to cut that part of the snake where the bile is extracted, and this is added directly to wine in the glass ready to be served.

There is the Elixir of Life wine made from a root which is found on the border of the mountains of Manchuria and Korea. It is the Korean people who make the most of this root which is exported around the world under the name of Ginseng. The most valuable are the three-pronged, creamy coloured roots. There are many grades and colours, the clearer the more valuable. In the Chinese opera, where lead singers are required to remain on stage for very long periods, the singers take Ginseng in dry or in liquid form to help with their breathing and give them the stamina required to perform.

Since the founding of New China, a brand of beer from the Laoshan Springs near the coastal city of Tsingtao has been produced with home-grown hops. This is mainly made for export purposes.

WINES TO SERVE WITH CHINESE FOOD

When you have acquired the expertise to plan a Chinese dinner for home entertaining, you may wonder what drinks to serve apart from Chinese wines. I list below a table of suggestions that should combine well with Chinese food. Firstly, let me remind you that in the Chinese cuisine there are many flavourings and subtle combinations and the whole meal will consist of many contrasts of tastes and texture. For instance, there will be sweet and sour, soft and crispy, salty and spicy, mild and sweet, bitter and sweet and soup-type dishes. Therefore, in the choosing of your wine, there should be one that complements all these flavours.

Dishes	Suggested wine
Hors d'oeuvre	Champagne cocktails Dry sherry Sweet sherry Cream sherry Martinis Sparkling wines
Fish and Seafood	Champagne White wines Dry sherry Sparkling wines
Vegetables	Sweet sherry Dry sherry Sparkling wines Light white wine
Chicken and Pork	Champagne White wines Sparkling wines Muscat Dry sherry Gin
Duck and Game Birds	Champagne Burgundy Claret Sparkling burgundy

	Brandy
	Whisky
Dessert	Liqueurs
	Cognac
	Brandy

If you are invited to attend a banquet at a restaurant where there will be at least ten to fourteen courses, it is unwise to choose beer or ale to drink between courses, because it will spoil your taste for the following dishes. I suggest you choose the wines of your choice to sip between courses and finish with Liqueurs and brandy. *Yum Sing!*

NORTHERN CHINA WINES

Fen Chiew　汾 酒

A dry wine made from millet. This is considered to be a fairly expensive one.

Mei Kuei　玫瑰露酒

A very popular dry liqueur; not very strong but has a very nice flavour. It is made from a grain known as Kao Liang (a grain golden in colour about the size of a grain of sago) and from corn.

Kiao Liang Chiew　高粱酒

A popular dry white wine, which is rather mild. It is served for guests at parties and celebrations in the north where it is very cold. It is made from the Kiao Liang grain and is very intoxicating. It is not unlike gin.

Wu Chia Pi Chiew　五加皮酒

A sweet very strong wine (about 96% proof). It is used a lot for medicinal purposes. Also very popular at high class parties for proposing toasts to special guests. It is made from Kao Liang with a very light essence of caramel. It is considered an expensive wine.

Chu Yeh Ching Chiew　竹葉清酒

A sweet, medium strength wine. It is clear and made from millet. It is fairly popular for the middle income class, as it is inexpensive.

Wai Sang Chiew　衛生酒

A sweet mild wine. It is made from rice and is also popular for the middle income group because of its price. (Rice wine is heated in special porcelain pots first and then served in tiny cups and sipped between courses.)

Moutai Chiew 茅台酒

This is the internationally famous Chinese liqueur named after the town in which it is produced. It is a clear, mellow one with a full bouquet containing 53% alcohol (106 proof). In the Moutai district the climate is moist and warm and has an abundance of rain and mist. The town lies in a gorge between high mountains on the Yunnan-Kweichow Plateau and the Chishui River flows past the town with water so clear that one can see the river-bed. It is here under these ideal conditions that the fermenting for Moutai is perfected. Choice sorghum and yeast prepared from carefully selected wheat go into the preparation of Moutai. It is a very popular toasting and celebration wine and as its popularity grows, it is fast taking its rightful place as a fine liqueur being served at banquets and cocktail parties in many countries of the world.

SOUTHERN CHINA WINES

Fa Diew Chiew 花雕酒

A dry medium bodied wine, amber coloured. It is served warm and used mostly during the winter months. Its main base is rice.

Nor Mei Chiew 糯米酒

This comes in two types, white and yellow. It is a dry very strong wine and used in the cooking of game and game birds. The women folk drink the wine after having given birth, as they believe this wine has the quality of helping them regain their health and strength. It is made from glutinous rice.

Sam Jing Chiew 三蒸酒

A dry medium strength wine, colourless. This is served for sipping between courses at banquets. It is made from rice but distilled three times.

Sheung Jing Chiew 双蒸酒

A dry medium strength wine, amber coloured. This is served for sipping between courses at banquets. It is made from rice but distilled twice.

Mei Kuei Lu Chiew 玫瑰露酒

A fragrant wine because of the addition of special rose petal essence. It is used extensively in cooking. It is very strong, 96% proof. This remarkable beverage, which is colourless, is made from Kios Liang and specially grown roses. It is suitable for all occasions as a very pleasant and refreshing drink.

Ng Ga Pei 五加皮酒

This is one of the Cantonese wines and is a dark amber colour, flavoured with herbs. Ng Ga Pei is bottled in a distinctive dark-brown porcelain jar with a wide lip and makes an ideal gift for special occasions. This wine may be used as the equivalent to brandy.

Charng Far Chiew 柑花酒

A liqueur distilled from grains of Kao Liang and flavoured with orange essence. There are other liqueurs made from peach, pear, plums, melon, lotus flowers, and apricots.

MEDICINAL WINES

Kee Kuk Chiew 杞菊酒

A reddish coloured herbal wine. It is made from chrysanthemums and a reddish seed from a herbal plant, all of which are ground together and mixed with distilled rice and allowed to ferment. It is prescribed for anyone after an operation where loss of blood occurs and helps to build up the system again.

Hop Gay Chiew 蛤蚧酒

This is a clear colour tonic wine. It is made from a rice base and frog essence. This is one of the wines taken as an antidote for stopping bed wetting.

Foo Gwat–Mook Gwah Bhiew 虎骨木瓜酒

This is a tonic wine used for strengthening one's blood. It is also useful in giving pep to one's body and aids virility. It is made from the finely ground bones of the tiger mixed with papaya juice and fermented rice.

Sarm Tse Chiew 三蛇酒

This tonic wine is made from three types of snake, one carpet and two black type snakes, mixed with fermented rice. This tonic when taken in the winter increases the heat in the body and is much revered in the cold winter months.

Loong Chiew 龍虎白鳳酒

Although the name of this wine means 'dragon wine' it is made with finely ground tiger bones and the white flesh of the white peacock, mixed with a rice base. This tonic is prescribed for anyone who is recuperating after a long sickness.

Gai Chiew 班豹烏腳酒

This is a tonic wine made from specially bred chickens. Only the legs of the chicken are used and it is mixed with rice and allowed to mature. This is a tonic for anyone who is feeling tired and suffers from loss of energy.

Jun Jee Fun Chiew 真珠酒

This one is only for the ladies. It is made from natural pearls. The pearl is finely ground and mixed with a Kao Liang wine. This wine is taken in the belief that a woman's youthful appearance will be preserved.

Shen Yuan Pu Chiu 參元補酒

This valuable tonic has as one of its ingredients the Ginseng root. It is taken as a tonic for preservation of good health. As the taste is sweet, it is quite pleasant to take.

Ling Pei 荃貝雪梨酒

This is made from the pears of China and is more a type of syrup for relieving coughs and colds. Water is used to dilute this syrup before using, as it is very rich on its own.

Chu Hua Chiew 菊花酒

This wine has white chrysanthemum petals added during the distillation process and is a mild type of wine which was formerly enjoyed by the warlords and Emperors only.

Huo Luo Chiew 活絡酒

A wine made of sorghum with the addition of prescribed herbs. It is amber coloured and, being mild in nature, can be served as a daily beverage.

Ginseng Chiew 人參酒

The Elixir of Life wine from the north-east province of China. It is well-known as a valuable tonic by the medicine men of all centuries in China. Dr. Li Shi-chen, the great Chinese scientist of medicine of the Ming dynasty, claimed in his book 'Outline of Herb Medicine', that Ginseng was the most efficient remedy for general weakness of both men and women. Even the scientist of this modern age acclaim this wine for its therapeutic value.

GLOSSARY OF CHINESE INGREDIENTS

Arrowroot: The plant is native to the West Indies and South America and also to Queensland, Australia. The rhizomes are peeled, washed, crushed and strained, and the starch is allowed to settle out. The name 'arrowroot' is derived from the Brazilian word for flour, *aru-aru*. Arrowroot is used for thickening soups and sauces and also in cakes.

Bamboo shoots (dook soon): Only the young shoots are used for food. The skin is scraped and the bamboo shoot is boiled until soft. It has a definite bamboo flavour. One may have to cultivate a taste for this vegetable. A canned variety, plain or flavoured, is available.

Bark gwor: This is the small fruit from the ginkgo-tree. It is about half an inch long and oval in shape. Its pale-cream outside shell is very soft, and, when cracked, reveals a small, soft, white nut encased in a brown skin. The nut is rather sweet and raw in flavour, but improves when added to soups and other dishes.

Bean curd (foo jook): This is a creamy-coloured food with a brittle texture, the dry form of bean curd. It is available in thin sheets or in long sticks, which must be soaked before use. When added to a dish, it becomes softer and has an elastic-like texture. It has a slightly burnt taste, to which the palate grows accustomed. It is used extensively in vegetarian dishes for fasting.

Bean curd (taofu): This is the equivalent of the Western cream cheese although it has a completely different flavour. It is made from the soy bean liquor and is rich in proteins and minerals. It is creamy in colour and has a bland smooth texture, with a slightly burnt flavour. It comes fresh and canned. It can be steamed, fried, deep-fried, braised and added to soups.

Bird's nest (yin wor): Soak in water overnight, then clean thoroughly and use tweezers to pluck off any tiny feathers that may have become stuck to the gelatine-like bird's nest. It is used in soup and considered a necessary delicacy in any banquet menu. When sweetened, it is served as a dessert.

Black beans (dow see): These beans are available in cans or in their preserved state. They are extremely salty black soy beans and, in their dry state, must be washed to rid them of any dust and excess salt. The odour is rather peculiar, but when these beans are cooked with seafood, meat or chicken, the bouquet and flavour are entirely different, and people become addicted to their taste. If canned beans are used, there is no need to wash them. They will keep indefinitely in a covered container. Use them sparingly in dishes. The dehydrated appearance belies the succulent flavour that these beans impart upon cooking.

Brown beans (min see jeung): This is a sweet bean sauce, purchased in small cans or jars. It consists of yellow soy beans, mixed with spices and seasonings. The beans are usually semi-crushed and impart a distinctive flavour when added to steamed fish and meat dishes. This sauce will keep indefinitely in the refrigerator.

Button mushrooms (champignons): These are small beige-coloured mushrooms about three-quarters of an inch in diameter. They enhance the appearance of a dish. Their use in Chinese dishes is increasing because they are becoming more plentiful. They are obtainable in cans and in frozen packs ready for immediate use.

Celery cabbage (wong ah bark): This is a delicate-green, thickly packed, long cabbage with white stems. It is used in all types of dishes, including soup, and has a rather sweet flavour. It can be used raw in a salad. Also known as Tiensin cabbage.

Cellophane noodles (fun see): Fine transparent bean starch noodles. Different processes of cooking produce different textures. When soaked in water they become limp, and if plunged into hot oil they immediately puff up and form a white, crisp mass of noodles.

Chili sauce (lart jew jeung): Made from small hot chilis. Beware if you are not accustomed to hot tastes, for this is quite a fiery one. It is used as a dip sauce for noodle dishes and meat dishes. A good substitute is tabasco, although the flavour is totally different.

Chinese cabbage (bark choy): This is a delicate cabbage with jade-green leaves and white stems. When it matures, a small bunch of yellow flowers appears at the top. Every part of the vegetable is used. It does not require long cooking and can be bought almost all the year round. This cabbage is also available in its dry state and is used extensively in soups.

Chinese flour (deng min fun): A special type of flour with a high gluten content, obtainable at Chinese delicatessens. It has a strong, elastic-like texture when mixed with water.

Chinese mustard top (guy choy): This is a cabbage with a strong green stem and slightly wavy, deep-green leaves. It has a bitter-sweet taste and is used in soups. When this cabbage is preserved in brine, it changes to a burnt-green colour and is extremely salty. The excess salt is washed out and the cabbage is cut into shreds or small pieces and cooked with meats; it is then called *sin choy*.

Chinese parsley (yin say): This is known as coriander and can very easily be grown in your own garden. It is a small, delicate, green-leaf plant which imparts a highly flavoured taste and a delightful aroma to a dish. The young green leaves are used as a garnish or in a salad, and the long green stalks are used in stock or for flavouring. When the plant has grown old, there is a light-purplish flower before it seeds. These seeds can be gathered and used. When the plant is watered, you can experience that marvellous aroma. No wonder it is favoured as a garnish for Chinese food.

Fermented bean curd (taofu): This is bean curd cut into cubes, fermented, dried in the sun and then steamed until tender. Bottled in wine and artificially coloured red or left plain creamy white, it has a tangy flavour.

Fish stomach (yue too); This is actually the stomach lining which has been dehydrated. It becomes hard when dried and looks like a transparent tyre tube rolled together. It must be soaked first in preparation for a soup. After it is cooked, it is cut up into chunks and becomes quite pulpy. There is very little taste to it, but, combined with other foods, the fish stomach absorbs other flavours.

Five spice powder (heung lo fun): Obtainable in small packets, this consists of a mixture of five spices. They are: Chinese aniseed, cloves, cinnamon, anise herb, and the aromatic seeds of fennel. The spice powder gives a wonderful aroma to food while it is cooking. This famous and well-known blend of five spices is considered by the Chinese to be a masterpiece of blending, and the dishes using this spice include chicken and pork. It should be used with discretion as it is not intended to overwhelm the flavours in a dish, but has the ability of making a simple dish into one in the gourmet class.

Fungi (chee yee): Greyish-black in colour and wrinkled. When soaked in cold water for fifteen minutes they expand to their fullest extent, and have an elastic-like quality. Wash well and use in numerous dishes where they can absorb the flavour of richer foods.

Garlic (sin tow): In form, garlic is a bulb similar to an onion but it can be broken away in separate cloves. It can be chopped finely, crushed or pressed to release the juice, and is used to flavour Chinese dishes.

Ginger (geung): The young root of a tropical plant which is used extensively in Chinese cooking. For best results, it requires good soil and drainage and is generally grown on slopes, heavily mulched with sawdust. When used in cooking seafood, it masks fishy odours and is versatile enough to enhance other foods. The Chinese belief that ginger is the essence of eternal youth comes from one of the oldest Chinese classics. This fresh root ginger is now obtainable in tins. There is also sugared ginger and ginger preserved in sweet syrup, both so popular for dessert. If fresh root ginger is unobtainable, use ginger in syrup, washing off the syrup first, then slicing up the ginger. Sometimes a pinch of ginger powder will give a ginger flavour to the dish requiring it, but fresh ginger root is best in most Chinese dishes.

Glutinous rice: A short grain rice which is very sticky. It is also known as sticky rice and is used extensively in making Chinese desserts. Store as for ordinary rice. There is also a flour ground from this rice which is used for desserts or for thickening purposes. It is used as a stuffing for poultry dishes also.

Golden needles (gum jum): This light-brown dried stem of the lily plant has a pleasant aromatic flavour when prepared and added to a dish. I tie one in a mystic knot and cook it with steamed chicken, which adds a very exotic touch to the presentation.

Hoisin sauce (hoisin jeung): It is a dark brown, sweet sauce obtainable in cans or jars. It is made from soy beans, sugar, spices, hot chilis, garlic and ginger root. It is known as the Chinese barbecue sauce. It is used extensively in the cooking of pork and poultry dishes and also as a dip sauce for Peking Duck, Roast Pork and Spare Ribs. It can be used in any recipe calling for sweet bean paste. It comes in salty and sweet flavours and stores indefinitely in a cool part of the refrigerator.

Lemon sauce: A lemon chutney used as an accompaniment to red roast pork or barbecued duck. In recent times Lemon Sauce Chicken has become a favourite, and this is the particular lemon sauce which gives the desired flavour required in this recipe.

Loong narn: The fresh loong narn is about three-quarters of an inch in diameter and the skin is smooth and round. When peeled, it reveals a luscious, sweet white flesh and a dark-brown seed. This fruit is related to the lychee but is usually more expensive, and some prefer it. It is obtainable canned, seeded and preserved in a light, sweet syrup and also in dried form with or without the shell. In the dried form it is used for medicinal soups and sweet dishes. It is also known as dragon's eyes or dragon seeds.

Lotus (ling kno):   This is cultivated in southern Asia and in the northern part of Australia. Every part of the plant can be used. The seeds or nuts are taken when slightly unripe. When ripe, they are cooked after the extremely bitter embryo is removed. The rhizomes are cooked with other foods and impart a unique flavour. They are also made into a kind of arrowroot. The stems *(gum jum)* can be eaten as well. The root or underwater stem of this lily plant has its own natural perforations running through its entire length, and when cut it looks attractive as it forms an interesting pattern.

Lotus nut (lin jee): These little nuts, products of the lotus plant, have a delicate flavour of their own. When pureed with sweetening added they are known as lotus nut paste, which is available in cans these days. Often on festive occasions lotus nuts are used in various dishes. The Chinese regard them as a symbol of fertility. Lotus flour, made from these nuts, is used as a thickening agent.

Lychee fruit: The fresh lychee is one to one and a half inches in diameter and it has a soft reddish skin which is easily peeled away, leaving a luscious, juicy, sweet white flesh and a large brown seed. When in season, the fresh fruit is sold on its branch and is very inexpensive. When they are dried, the shell becomes brittle, and the white flesh turns dark brown and shrivels on the seed. In this form it can be boxed and sent to every part of the world, and one need not be without lychee nuts (as they are known). Lychees, preserved in a light syrup, are available in cans and are a very good substitute for the fresh fruit.

Mandarin skin (gom pei): The mandarin skin is cut from the fruit in four sections, leaving the bottom part intact so that the skin falls away in one piece. The best skins come from the large, flat, brightly coloured fruit. The skins are threaded on twine and allowed to dry in the warm sun for three or four days and then kept in an airtight container until ready for use in different dishes. Mandarin skin lends full flavour, when soaked first, to chicken, meat and duck dishes. It is used whole in long-cooking dishes and then removed; used in other dishes, it is cut into strips. The Chinese believe that when the dried mandarin skin is soaked in hot water and allowed to cool, it can be applied as a medicine to those tiny irritations that occur at the corner of the mouth.

Melon seeds (gwah jee): These are the seeds from the melon; they are black or red and of varying sizes. When they are removed from the melon, they are dried, salted and spiced; they can then be toasted in a slow oven. They are very popular with the Chinese, who nibble them at parties, but you must have strong teeth to extract the tiny white kernel from the shell. The kernels are used in different types of cakes, pastries and candies. Pumpkin seeds are treated in the same way, but the outside skin is softer.

Monosodium glutamate (mee jing): This is marketed under various trade names and is of vegetable origin. Used very sparingly and with discretion, it enhances the natural flavour of foods. The Chinese version is a fine white powder called *ve-tsin.* It is one of the ingredients in stock cubes, so if you use a stock base, it is not necessary to add any extra to the dish that you are preparing. I find that after attending a banquet in a restaurant the effect of monosodium glutamate in every dish is to make me very thirsty.

Mushrooms, dried (doong gwoo): Obtainable in Asian countries, the best are said to come from Japan. They are grey to black in colour and come in varying thicknesses; from thick-centred mushrooms (considered first grade) to thin ones that are split on the edges and resemble a flower. They are available in sizes from very small to large. Soak all types of dried mushrooms in warm water for twenty minutes, when they will expand to their fullest extent. Wash and clean thoroughly, then soak in a second bowl of water, which can be retained and used as stock. When ready to use, squeeze the mushrooms dry and remove the stems (these can also be used in the stockpot). *See also* Button mushrooms.

Olive nuts (larm yin): This is the soft kernel of the Chinese olive and is used in various dishes that require a nutty texture.

Oyster sauce (hor yo): Made from Chinese oysters, this sauce imparts an exotic and individual flavour to dishes. It adds distinction to the food. It comes in different degrees of concentrated form, from thin to thick.

Plum sauce (mui jeung): Made from Chinese plums and apricots, it has a sweet-sour taste and can be used as any ordinary type of dip sauce. It usually accompanies roast duck.

Red bean curd (hoong narm yue): A soy bean product, obtainable in cans and jars. The red colour is artificial. Superb in pork dishes that require long cooking.

Assorted Chinese ingredients. Row 1, from left to right: Almond biscuits, prawns. Row 2: Red beans, chestnuts, salt vegetables, fungi, lotus nuts. Row 3: Olive nuts, Chinese black olives, golden needles, mandarin skin. Row 4: Red dates, lotus, pearlshell meat, reconstituted fungi. Row 5: Mushrooms, crab apple, fresh water chestnuts, scallops. Row 6: Sheet seaweed, shark's fin, star anise, prawns, chestnuts, maidenhair (seaweed).

Red bean puree (hoong do sar): This is a thick puree made from the natural red soy bean. It is made into a sweet filling and put into a yeast bun and the ever popular *jin doih.* The latter is made with glutinous rice flour, the sweet filling placed inside, and then deep-fried.

Red dates (hoong joh): These are dried and must be soaked in hot water for at least thirty minutes before using them in various dishes; except, of course, in the case of soup, when they are washed and added to the soup ingredients to simmer. They are also candied and used as dessert. The taste is a pleasant, sweet one, although the skin is a little tough and should be discarded along with the seed.

Rice wine (mei jow): Made from fermented rice, it is very similar to sherry; it is warmed before drinking. (See wine list.)

Salted fish (harm yue): This is fish preserved by salting and drying in the sun, usually without cutting through the stomach. When cooked, it is eaten as an appetizer. The commerical variety comes preserved in oil. It is extremely salty and, steamed with fresh ginger or minced pork, this humble dish is transformed into quite a meal for a gastronome. When salmon (*mar yo*) is preserved by this method, it is acclaimed by Cantonese as being *the* Prince of them all. Another method of presenting this salted fish is to dry-fry it in very little oil and then cut it into sections.

Salted vegetable (choong choy): Preserved salted vegetable usually obtainable in squat deep-brown earthenware jars which come in very handy later on for decoration. The fresh vegetable has a hard bulb from which grows a green stem. Every part of this vegetable is used in the preserving process.

Sartee sauce (sartee jup): This is a pourable sauce, rich brown in colour, made from soy beans and spices, with a sprinkling of chilis. It is available in bottles under various brand names and is used for chicken and meat sartees as a variation from the hotter chilli sauces.

Today the 'sartee' or 'sate' dishes are a popular addition to restaurant menus under names such as Prawns Sate or Beef Sate. These dishes are cooked in the bottled sate sauce as a main ingredient. Before using, it is advisable to stir the sauce thoroughly as the vegetables and the spices separate in the bottle.

Scallops, dried (gong yo jee): Soak whole scallops in warm water for eight hours, when they will be easy to shred. They are used extensively in soup and omelettes. Scallops can be eaten as an appetizer.

Assorted noodles. Top left: Sar hor fun, made from rice flour. Middle: Noodles made from wheat, uncooked (white and green), deep fried (left), cooked in boiling water (right) and as used in soups (top right). Bottom left: The fine Fukien noodles. Bottom right: Mei fun, made from rice flour.

Seaweed (faht choy): The very fine black threads of seaweed are used in fasting dishes by Buddhists. They must be washed thoroughly and then soaked and cooked with other food, when they become soft and glossy, but retain their black colour. It certainly is an experience for anyone who has not tasted *faht choy* before. The dried, thin sheets of seaweed, known as *hoi dye*, are dark purple in colour and are rich in calcium and protein. They are used in soups and braised dishes. They too have an unusual flavour. The Japanese roll up rice and spices in these sheets and then steam them; they are then cut into sections and eaten cold.

Sesame (jee mar): This herb has small, oval seeds. They are used for food and, when toasted, are a delightful addition to cakes, bread and salads. They are obtainable in different colours, including black.

Sesame oil (jee mar yo): A highly refined, fragrant oil obtained from the sesame seed; it keeps indefinitely in bottles. It should be used sparingly when added to dishes.

Sesame paste (jee mar jeung): This is a paste comparable to the texture of peanut paste and is used as a flavouring in steamed or braised foods. It is highly concentrated, so must be used sparingly. It is obtainable in tins or jars and usually lasts quite a while, since a teaspoon at a time is all that is necessary in a dish.

Shallots (choong): The shallot is also known as scallion or spring onion, depending on usage in different parts of the world. Shallots are usually sold in bunches. They have a small bulb and a narrow green shoot, all of which can be used. In some Far Eastern countries the shallot is described as a bulb-like root with a purplish skin. The Chinese call the long thin green type the winter shallot and the larger, longer green type the summer shallot. In endeavouring to simplify my text, I have referred to all types as shallots.

Shark's fin (yue chee): This is actually the fin of the shark and is dried. It is prepared by cleaning and removing the skin, and is then boiled for anything up to ten days, when a translucent gelatine substance is extracted. It is prized greatly by the Chinese and is the supreme delicacy on a banquet menu (its only rival being bird's nest soup); it is also revered for its high vitamin content. Shark's fin can be purchased in its semi-processed form, which shortens the cooking time. Instant shark's fin soup is available in tins.

Shrimp-prawn crisps (har beang): Also known as prawn biscuit, these are made from shrimps and prawns, and when they are dried in the sun they become very brittle. They are obtainable in different sizes, ranging from 2.5 cm to 15 cm long, and the smaller ones are treated with vegetable colouring. Also the shapes are varied, from long oval to round. When cooked in deep oil they expand and, when cool, become very crisp. They can be kept in an airtight container and eaten as a titbit. The large variety can be used as a substitute for a slice of bread or a pancake; crushed, it can be sprinkled on a salad.

Shrimp paste (harm har): This is made from tiny shrimps, and it takes thousands to make up one small bottle. This paste has a strong fishy odour and is purplish in colour, and one has to acquire a taste for it. It is used very sparingly. A small dish of it steamed with rice while it is cooking is served as an appetizer to the lovers of this paste.

Shrimps, dried (har mei): Soak in warm water for one hour or longer. These are used as a substitute for fresh shrimps, but are inclined to be salty. They are most desirable for use in omelettes and soups.

Soy sauce: Made from salted and fermented soy beans. No Chinese kitchen is ever without it. There are different grades, ranging from thin to thick, and the colour varies from light brown to dark reddish-brown. It may be used during the cooking process and is always set on the table as a dip sauce, just as salt and pepper would take its place on a Western table. Though salty, soy sauce is not a complete substitute for salt. The cooking variety, which is light in colour, is called *sarng chow*; the table variety is called *see yo*.

Squid, dried (yew yue): Soak in warm water for one hour or longer. Wash thoroughly, removing any sand and taking particular care to clean the tendrils. Peel off the skin and cut a criss-cross pattern on the inside. When cooked, the squid will curl into an attractive, patterned log shape. Squid are excellent fare when steamed and are used in dishes combined with vegetables.

Star anise (bart gock): This is a spice which has eight petals arranged like a daisy and its colour is deep brown. It is capable of imparting a very strong flavour to whatever it comes into contact with, so use sparingly.

Sweet paste (mor see jeung): It is made from soy beans and spices, then sweetened. It comes under different brand names, either in jars or cans. Why not try the different brands to explore the difference it makes to your cooking.

Taro (wu): Taro is cultivated throughout the tropics for its edible starchy tuberous rhizomes. It belongs to the arum lily family and is related to elephant's ear. The tuberous rhizomes must be treated by boiling, baking or roasting.

Water chestnut (mar tay): This annual waterplant with fruits like a buffalo head is native to China and cultivated also in Japan and Formosa. It is used in various dishes and is creamy white when the black–brown skin is peeled from the fruit, and the texture is very sweet and crisp. It is also preserved in honey and candied. The seeds of the plant can also be made into flour and used for thickening purposes.

White bean curd (narm yue): Made from soy bean, salted and used as an appetizer or combined with vegetable dishes. Usually comes in 2.5 cm blocks, in jars, or canned.

INDEX